AMERICAN NATURE GUIDES

# FRESHWATER FISH

To my father on
his 74th birthday
Love
Christine Jay

AMERICAN NATURE GUIDES

# FRESHWATER FISH

HENRY W. ROBISON

SMITHMARK

This edition first published by
SMITHMARK Publishers Inc.,
112 Madison Avenue, New York 10016

© Copyright: 1992 Dragon's World Ltd
© Copyright: 1992 Text Henry W. Robison
© Copyright: 1992 Illustrations Richard Bell, Tony Gibbons,
David More, Robert Morton, Colin Newman, all of
Bernard Thornton Artists, London

Published in England by Dragon's World Ltd,
Limpsfield and London

Editor: Diana Steedman
Designer: Carole Perks
Art Director: Dave Allen
Editorial Director: Pippa Rubinstein

SMITHMARK Books are available for bulk purchase for sales
promotions and premium use. For details write or telephone
the Manager of Special Sales, SMITHMARK Publishers Inc.,
112 Madison Avenue,
New York, New York 10016. (212) 532-6600

ISBN 0 8317 6968 8

Printed in Singapore

# Contents

# Introduction

Fishes are the most successful and amazingly diverse group of vertebrate animals on Earth, with estimates of the number of living species ranging from 18,000 to over 40,000. Most recent estimates set the number at about 21,500. These species are divided into approximately 36 orders and more than 450 families. Fishes total more than half of all living vertebrate species. Living fishes may be classified into three main groups; the jawless fishes (lampreys and hagfishes), the cartilaginous fishes (sharks, skates, and rays), and the bony fishes.

The North American fish fauna is represented by more than 2200 species of fishes of which approximately 950 species inhabit fresh water. The greatest diversity in North American freshwater fishes appears in two dominant families: Cyprinidae (carps and minnows) – 280 species, and Percidae (perches and darters) – 150 species, although Catostomidae (suckers – *c.*60 species), Cyprinodontidae (killifishes – *c.*50 species), Ictaluridae (catfishes – 39 species), and Centrarchidae (sunfishes and basses – 29 species) make up a significant number of North American freshwater species. A number of families including Polyodontidae (paddlefishes), Amiidae (bowfin), Anguillidae (freshwater eels), Aphredoderidae (pirate perches), and Sciaenidae (drums) are represented in North America by a single freshwater species each.

Fishes exhibit tremendous variation in morphology, behavior and ecology with members of the most advanced group, the Teleostei, having penetrated virtually every aquatic habitat, ranging from ocean depths of 38,000ft (11,000m) to high mountains of 14,500ft (4500m)) and hot springs (109°F (43°C)) to subfreezing water (28°F (-2°C)).

**Geographical Area Covered**
This is a field guide to over 300 of the most common, abundant, and interesting freshwater fishes in 31 families occurring in North America north of Mexico. Some anadromous species are treated, such as certain

salmon, which spend part of their lives at sea, then return to fresh water to spawn. Also included are a few species, notably killifishes or topminnows, which inhabit both estuarine and freshwater environments. Although the book emphasizes native fish species, certain long-established and more recently introduced species are included. A companion volume in this field guide series covers saltwater fishes of North America.

## How to Use This Guide

The guide covers two classes of fishes which generally occur in the fresh waters of North America: the jawless lampreys, and the more numerous bony fishes. Within a family, the genera and species are arranged alphabetically by scientific name. Use of common and scientific names of fishes and their order of appearance follows the sequence adopted by the American Fisheries Society in their 1990 *List of Common and Scientific Names of Fishes from the United States and Canada.*

Emphasis is placed on identification of fishes in the field when they are freshly caught or seen underwater. Important distinguishing or "field" characters are provided in the text and illustrated on the plates of the respective species. No scientific key to the identification of all freshwater species covered in this guide is provided due to space constraints and the necessity of a much more technical background to facilitate the use of such a key. Instead, the reader should look through the book to find the fish or group of fishes which resemble the specimen in question. Read the text portion carefully for additional confirming characters. Examine the illustration of the species to verify your decision.

All 307 species of freshwater fishes described in the text are illustrated. Each species is depicted next to the respective text entry. The illustrations depict normal, daytime color and pattern for each species. Adults are used to provide the "norm" for the species as these will more commonly be encountered.

In addition to common and scientific names, identification characters are provided as is information describing the habitat and range for each species. For many species, additional comments are provided, noting various aspects of the natural history of the species.

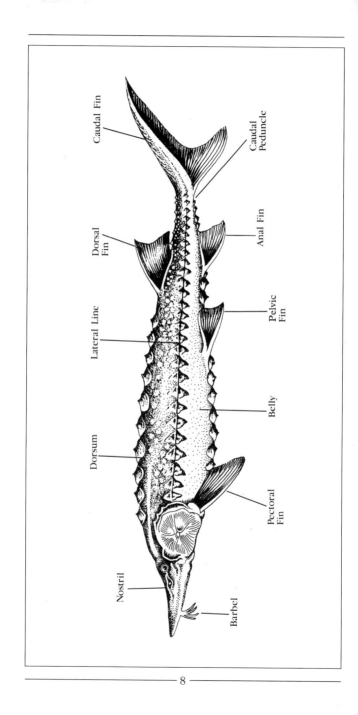

Caudal Fin

Caudal Peduncle

Anal Fin

Dorsal Fin

Pelvic Fin

Lateral Line

Belly

Dorsum

Pectoral Fin

Nostril

Barbel

# Glossary

**Abbreviate-Heterocercal** Type of caudal fin found in gars in which the posterior end of the vertebral column is distinctly curved upward and partially enters the upper half of the fin.

**Adipose Fin** A small, fleshy, rayless fin located on the midline of the back between the dorsal and caudal fins in catfishes, salmonids, and some other fishes.

**Ammocoete** Larval stage of lampreys.

**Anadromous** A fish that spawns and spends its early life in fresh water but moves into the ocean where it attains sexual maturity and spends most of its life span, as in the Alabama shad.

**Anal Fin** Median, ventral unpaired fin situated posterior to the anus.

**Anterior** Relating to the front.

**Anus** The exterior opening of the digestive tract; the vent.

**Axillary Process** A long, thin, membranous flap or modified scale at the anterior base of the pelvic fins in the Hiodontidae and Salmonidae, and at the anterior bases of both the pectoral and pelvic fins in the Clupeidae and Mugilidae.

**Barbel** A slender, elongate, flexible process located near the mouth, snout, and chin areas; tactile and gustatory in function.

**Basicaudal** Area at the base of the caudal fin.

**Belly** Ventral surface posterior to the base of the pelvic fins and anterior to the anal fin.

**Benthic-dwelling** Living on the bottom.

**Branched Ray** A soft ray which is forked or branched away from its base.

**Branchiostegal Ray** One of the elongate, flattened bones supporting the gill membranes, ventral to the operculum.

**Breast** Ventral surface in front of the pelvic fins; anterior to the belly.

**Canine Teeth** Sharp, conical teeth in the front part of the jaws; conspicuously larger than the rest of the teeth.

**Cartilaginous** Skeleton composed of cartilage.

**Catadromous** A fish, such as the American eel, that grows to sexual maturity in fresh water but migrates to the ocean to spawn.

**Caudal Fin** Tail fin.

**Caudal Peduncle** The narrow region of the body in front of the caudal fin from the posterior end of the base of the anal fin to the base of the caudal fin.

**Cheek** The area between the eye and the preopercle bone.

**Circumpolar** Found in polar regions.

**Cleithrum bone** Major bone of the pectoral girdle.

**Ctenoid Scales** Thin scales that bear a patch of tiny spine-like prickles (ctenii) on the exposed (posterior) surface.

**Cuspid** A tooth with one cusp (see **bicuspid** and **multicuspid**).

**Cycloid Scales** More or less rounded scales that are flat and bear no ctenii.

**Distal** Farthest from point of attachment (e.g. free edge of fins, farthest from their bases).

**Dorsal** Referring to the back; used as an abbreviation for dorsal fin.

**Dorsum** The upper part of the body; the back.

**Elver** Young or immature eel.

**Emarginate** Having a distal margin notched, indented, or slightly forked.

**Falcate** A fin is said to be falcate when its margin is deeply concave or sickle-shaped.

**Filament** A thread-like process usually associated with the fins.

**Fin-Ray** A bony or cartilaginous rod supporting the fin membrane. Soft rays usually are segmented (cross-striated), often branched and flexible near their tips, whereas spines are not segmented, never branched, and usually are stiff to their sharp distal tips.

**Frenum** A ridge or fold of tissue that connects the upper lip to the snout.

**Ganoid Scales** Thick, strong rhombic scales with a covering of ganoin, as in gars.

**Gill Filaments** Respiratory structures projecting posteriorly from gill arches.

**Gill Membranes** Membranes that close the gill cavity ventrolaterally, supported by the branchiostegals.

**Gill Rakers** Projections (knobby or comb-like) from the concave anterior surface of the gill arches.

**Gonopodium** Modified, rod-like anal fin of male *Gambusia* used in the transfer of sperm to genital pore of female.

**Gular Plate** Large, median, dermal bone on the throat, as in the bowfin.

**Heterocercal** A type of tail of fishes in which the vertebral column turns upward into the dorsal lobe.

**Humeral Spot** Scale-like bone, often dark-colored, behind the gill opening and above the base of the pectoral fin (in darters).

**Inferior** Beneath, lower, or on the ventral side; e.g. inferior mouth.

**Infraorbital Canal** Segment of the lateral-line canal in the suborbital bones that curves beneath the eye and extends forward onto the snout; canal may be complete or interrupted.

**Keel** Scales or tissue forming a sharp edge or ridge.

**Lateral Line** System of sensory tubules communicating to the body surface by pores; refers most often to a longitudinal row of scales that bear tubules and visible pores; considered incomplete if only the anterior scales possess pores and complete if all scales in that row (to base of caudal fin) have pores.

**Leptocephalus** Larval eel.

**Lobes** Rounded projections.

**Maxilla (Maxillary)** A bone of each upper jaw that lies immediately above (or behind) and parallel to the premaxilla.

**Median** Relating to the middle.

**Myomere** Muscle segment.

**Non-protractile** Not protrusible; premaxillaries are non-protractile if they are not fully separated from the snout by a continuous groove.

**Ocellus** An eye-like spot, usually round with a light or dark border.

**Opercle** The large posterior bone of the gill cover; may be spiny, serrate, or entire (smooth).

**Operculum** Bony flap covering the gills of fishes, also called the gill cover.

**Origin (or fins)** Anterior end of the base of a dorsal fin or anal fin.

**Palatine Teeth** Teeth on the paired palatine bones which lie on the roof of the mouth.

**Papillose** Covered with small, nipple-like projections.

**Parr Marks** Nearly square or oblong blotches found along the sides of young trout before they have developed the adult color pattern.

**Pectoral Fin** The anteriormost paired fin on the side, or on the breast, behind the head.

**Pelagic** Of open waters; usually referring to lakes.

**Pelvic Fin** The ventral-paired fin, lying below the pectoral fin or below the pectoral fin or between it and the anal fin.

**Peritoneum** Membranous lining of the body cavity.

**Pharyngeal Teeth** Bony projections from the fifth pharyngeal (gill) arch.

**Plicate** Having parallel folds of soft ridges; grooved lips, especially prominent on the lips of certain catostomids.

**Posteriad** In a posterior direction.

**Predorsal Scales** Scales on the midline of the dorsum between the back edge of the head and the dorsal fin origin.

**Premaxilla (Premaxillary)** A paired bone at the front of the upper jaw. The right and left premaxillae join anteriorly and form all or part of the border of the jaw.

**Preopercle** Sickle-shaped bone lying behind and below the eye; may be serrated or smooth.

**Principal Rays** Fin-rays that extend to the distal margin of median fins; enumerated by counting only one unbranched ray anteriorly plus subsequent branched rays.

**Protractile** Capable of being thrust out, when the upper jaw is completely separated from the snout by a continuous groove (frenum absent).

**Proximal** Nearer the body; center or base of attachment.

**Pustulose** Having blister-like projections.

**Pyloric caeca** Finger-like, blind tubes at the junction of stomach and intestine.

**Recurved** Curved upward and inward.

**Saddle** Rectangular or linear bars or bands which cross the back and extend partially or entirely downward across the sides.

**Scapular bar** Bar in the shoulder region.

**Scute** A modified scale in the form of a horny or bony plate which is often spiny or keeled.

**Serrate** Toothed or notched on the edge, like a saw.

**Striations** Streaked or striped by narrow parallel lines or grooves.

**Subopercle** Bone immediately below the opercle in the operculum.

**Suborbital** Thin bone forming lower part of orbital rim.

**Supramaxilla** Small, wedge-shaped movable bone adherent to the upper edge of the maxilla near its posterior tip.

**Supraoral** Above the mouth.

**Supratemporal** Area near the occiput.

**Terete** Cylindrical and tapering with circular cross-section; having a rounded body form, the width and depth about equal.

**Terminal Mouth** When the upper and the lower jaws form the extreme anterior tip of the head.

**Thoracic** Pertaining to the chest region in fishes; pelvic fins thoracic when inserted below the pectoral fins.

**Tubercle** A small projection or lump; refers to keratinized or osseus structures developed during the breeding period, i.e. breeding tubercles.

**Venter** The belly or lower sides of a fish.

**Ventral** Pertaining to the lower surface.

**Vermiculate** Worm-like; marked with irregular or wavy lines.

**Vomer** A median bone, usually bearing teeth, at the anterior extremity of the roof of the mouth.

**Weberian Apparatus** A series of ossicles (small bones) that conduct vibrations or pressure changes from gas bladder to ear, involving the first 4 or 5 fused vertebrae behind the head.

# Lampreys – Petromyzontidae

Lampreys, also called "jawless fishes" because of their unique absence of jaws, are direct descendants of the earliest true fishes on Earth which first appeared over 400 million years ago. In North America, the family is represented by 17 species. Often called "lamprey-eels", lampreys are easily distinguished from true eels by the absence of true jaws, a single median nostril, cartilaginous skeleton, no scales, no paired fins, and seven pairs of gill pouches.

Lampreys occur in two separate stages as larvae (ammocoetes) and adults. Adults spawn in streams near the upper ends of gravelly riffles. Larval lampreys resemble adults, but lack the sucking disc, rasping teeth, eyes, and have a hood covering the mouth. Larvae undergo transformation into adults after one to three years, usually during the fall.

## Chestnut lamprey
*Ichthyomyzon castaneus*                                    20in (51cm)

**Identification** Brownish, eel-like body; jaws, paired fins, and scales absent; poorly developed eyes; seven gill openings. Dorsal fin not separated into two distinct parts. Cup-shaped mouth wider than head when expanded with well-developed horny teeth in radiating rows. Myomeres usually 52–56.
**Habitat** Rivers and large reservoirs.
**Range** Mississippi River system, Great Lakes, Mobile Bay drainage, and Red River.
**Comments** Parasitic species; feeds by attaching its disc-like mouth to host species with its horny tongue which rasps a hole in the host while an anticoagulant is injected into the wound to keep the blood and body fluids flowing.

# Southern brook lamprey
*Ichthyomyzon gagei*                                           5in (13cm)

**Identification** Non-parasitic; no jaws, paired fins, or scales. Poorly
developed eyes. Dorsal fin shallowly notched, but not separated into
two distinct parts. Expanded disc narrower than head. Myomeres
52–56.
**Habitat** Clear, permanent flowing small to medium-sized streams.
**Range** Gulf of Mexico drainage from Oklahoma and Texas north to
Missouri and east to Florida.
**Comments** Adults move to tributary streams in spring (April and
May) where they construct nests 6–8in (15–20cm) and about 2in
(5cm) deep in sand and gravel and spawn when water temperatures
reach 59–75°F (15–24°C)


# Least brook lamprey
*Lampetra aepyptera*                                           7in (18cm)

**Identification** Non-parasitic lamprey with a deeply notched dorsal fin
divided into two separate parts. Jaws, paired fins and scales absent.
One pair of prominent widely separated supraoral teeth. Eyes
prominent. Myomeres 55–60.
**Habitat** Headwater creeks and streams with clean gravel riffles.
**Range** Atlantic slope; west of Appalachians from Pennsylvania to
Ohio, south to Alabama and Mississippi, west to Arkansas and
Missouri.
**Comments** Adults spawn in streams less than 15ft (4.5m) wide when
water temperature reaches 50°F(10°C) from mid-March to mid-April.

## American brook lamprey
*Lampetra appendix*                                          8in (20cm)

**Identification** Non-parasitic lamprey; dorsal fin divided into two
separate parts. Mouth disc as wide as head. Few teeth in the marginal
fields of disc, moderately well developed, usually with three pairs of
bicuspids. Myomeres 66–75.
**Habitat** Headwater streams with clean gravel riffles.
**Range** Mississippi River system, St Lawrence basin, and from New
Hampshire to Roanoke River on Atlantic slope.


## Pacific lamprey
*Lampetra tridentata*                                        30in (76cm)

**Identification** Eel-like body. Jaws absent, broad tooth plate above
mouth with three rows, four pairs of lateral teeth. Paired fins absent,
dorsal fin divided into two parts. Myomeres 64–67. Parasitic.
**Habitat** Adults inhabit rivers, while ammocoetes prefer shallow
backwater and eddy areas.
**Range** Pacific Ocean from Alaska to southern California.
**Comments** Anadromous parasitic lamprey; spawns in April when
water reaches about 47°F (8°C). Ammocoetes transform at four to six
years old.


## Sea lamprey
*Petromyzon marinus*                                         34in (86cm)

**Identification** Parasitic lamprey; no jaws, paired fins or scales.
Mouth with numerous rasp-like teeth; eyes small. Seven gill openings.
Myomeres 67–74.
**Habitat** Coastal estuaries and enters fresh water.
**Range** Northern Florida to Gulf of St Lawrence.
**Comments** The sea lamprey circumvented Niagara Falls and entered
the Great Lakes where it originally decimated the fish population.

# Sturgeons – Acipenseridae

Sturgeons belong to a very primitive group of bony fishes which has seven species in North America. Sturgeons are characterized by an elongated body with a largely cartilaginous skeleton; an extended, hard snout; ventral protrusible mouth with four barbels; heterocercal tail; and heavy dermal plates arranged in five rows along the sides and dorsum.

## Shortnose sturgeon
*Acipenser brevirostrum*                                              36in (91cm)

**Identification** Short, bluntly rounded snout, four barbels, protrusible mouth, heterocercal tail, dorsal fin located far posterior over anal fin. Pelvic fins abdominal. Rows of large bony plates. Anal fin rays 19–22. Size to 9lbs (4kg).
**Habitat** Large tidal rivers, brackish and salt water.
**Range** Atlantic Coast from St John River in New Brunswick, Canada to St John's River, eastern Florida.

# Lake sturgeon
*Acipenser fulvescens*                                  9ft (2.4m)

**Identification** Large grayish sturgeon; snout conical. Tail heterocercal. Four barbels, smooth, not fringed, and subequal. Lower lip with two lobes.
**Habitat** Shallow shoal areas of lakes and the deepest portions of large rivers.
**Range** Hudson Bay west to Southern Alberta, Canada to St Lawrence estuary to Mississippi River system to Coosa River, Alabama.
**Comments** Adults mature at 14–20 years, occasionally reaching 150 years. Ranks as one of the largest freshwater fishes of North America.


# Green sturgeon
*Acipenser medirostris*                                 7ft (2.1m)

**Identification** Greenish; flattened snout, small protrusible mouth, heterocercal tail, a single row of one to four bony plates along the midventral line between the anus and the anal fin. Dorsal fin rays 33–35. Four sensory barbels anterior to mouth, their bases closer to mouth than to tip of snout. Anal fin rays 22–28.
**Habitat** Anadromous; commonly found in estuaries and lower reaches of large rivers.
**Range** Pacific Coast of North America from Alaska to southern California.

# Atlantic sturgeon
*Acipenser oxyrhynchus*                                          10ft (3m)

**Identification** A large, robust fish; long flattened snout. Four barbels
anterior to mouth midway between tip of snout and mouth, dorsal fin
far back, heterocercal tail, pelvics abdominal and rows of large bony
plates on sides. Four plates, usually as two pairs, between anal fin and
caudal fulcrum. Up to 300lbs (136kg).
**Habitat** Anadromous; large rivers.
**Range** Atlantic Coast from Labrador to eastern Florida.


# White sturgeon
*Acipenser transmontanus*                                       12½ft(3.8m)

**Identification** Large grayish sturgeon rounded in cross section,
flattened head, short broad snout, with four long barbels. Mouth
ventral. Midlateral plates 38–48. Heterocercal tail.
**Habitat** Large rivers.
**Range** Pacific slope from Aleutian Islands, Alaska south to Monterey,
California.
**Comments** Anadromous species. Ascends large rivers in spring to
spawn. Largest individuals probably live over 100 years and weigh
more than 100lbs (544kg). Over-fishing has led to a drastic decline in
populations.

# Pallid sturgeon
*Scaphirhynchus albus*

43in (1.1m)

**Identification** Pale sturgeon with a flattened, shovel-shaped snout. Belly without plates. Lower lip with four papillose lobes. Bases of outer barbels slightly farther back than bases of inner barbels; length of inner barbel short, about half the length of the outer.
**Habitat** Large, turbid rivers in strong current over a firm sand bottom.
**Range** Main channels of Missouri and lower Mississippi rivers.
**Comments** Food consists of small fishes and immature aquatic insects. Spawning occurs in June and July. Most adults reach 15–25lbs (6.8–11.3kg) with a maximum size of 68lbs (30.8kg)

# Shovelnose sturgeon
*Scaphirhynchus platorynchus*

36in (91cm)

**Identification** Small, buff or drab sturgeon with broad, flattened head. Four strongly fringed barbels; inner barbel much more than half length of the outer. Lower lip with four papillose lobes. Eye small. Rows of bony plates which converge on caudal peduncle. Belly covered with small scales. Anal rays 23 or fewer.
**Habitat** Shallow areas and deep channels of larger rivers, inhabiting sand bars or areas of strong current.
**Range** Mississippi and Missouri River system west to Rio Grande; Mobile Bay drainage, Alabama.
**Comments** Adults migrate upstream from April to early July to spawn over rocky substrate in channels of large rivers at water temperatures of 67–70°F (19–21°C).

# Paddlefishes – Polyodontidae

The American paddlefish, *Polyodon spathula* , is the only North American species in this Family. Characteristics include a paddle-like snout, a naked body except for a few minute ganoid scales on the upper lobe of the caudal fin, and a gill cover greatly extended posteriorly.

## Paddlefish
*Polyodon spathula*                                                7ft (21m)

**Identification** Bluish-gray fish with long, paddle-shaped snout, heterocercal tail, large mouth and small eyes. Body naked except for a few minute ganoid scales on upper lobe of caudal fin. Operculum produced into a long, pointed flap.
**Habitat** Large, low-gradient rivers occupying backwater areas; also in lowland, periodically flooded oxbow lakes.
**Range** Mississippi River system; Mobile Bay drainage, Alabama.
**Comments** One of North America's most primitive fishes. Lives up to 30 years and grows to 200lbs (91kg). It spawns from April-June. Fishermen catch them by snagging.

# Gars – Lepisosteidae

Gars are long, slender fishes with cylindrical bodies covered with plate-like ganoid scales, a snout produced into a distinctly elongated beak with many sharp teeth, and a rounded and abbreviate-heterocercal tail. There are seven living species of this primitive family, five of which occur in North America.

## Alligator gar
*Atractosteus spatula*                    10ft (3m)

**Identification** Large gar, snout short, broad. Teeth in upper jaw in two rows on each side. Ganoid scales. Abbreviate-heterocercal tail. Lateral line scales 58–62.
**Habitat** Sluggish pools and backwaters of large rivers, sometimes enters brackish and salt waters along the Gulf Coast.
**Range** Florida west along Gulf Coast to Veracruz, Mexico. Mississippi River north to Illinois and Ohio River in southern Ohio.
**Comments** Feeds mainly on fishes. Spawning occurs from April-June. One of the largest freshwater fishes in North America.

## Spotted gar
*Lepisosteus oculatus*                    36in (91cm)

**Identification** Dark spots on top of head, snout, body and fins. Snout short. Teeth in single row. Ganoid scales. Lateral line scales 53–59.
**Habitat** Quiet, clear pools of streams, swamps and lakes with heavy aquatic vegetation.
**Range** Great Lakes south to Gulf Coast; Mississippi River system from Illinois south to Oklahoma, west to Florida and Texas.
**Comments** Spawns in spring in shallow aquatic vegetation. Feeds primarily on fishes.

# Longnose gar
*Lepisosteus osseus*                                    6ft (1.8m)

**Identification** An elongate, brownish fish with a long slender snout.
Teeth in upper jaw in a single row. Top of head and snout without
spots. Ganoid scales. Abbreviate-heterocercal tail. Lateral line scales
57–63. Predorsal scales 47–55.
**Habitat** Inhabits rivers, bayous, oxbow lakes, and swamps.
**Range** Southern Quebec south to Florida, west to Great Lakes and
south to Rio Grande of Mexico.
**Comments** Feeds on fishes. Adults spawn in smaller tributaries in
spring. Spawning occurs over gravel or weedy areas from early May to
mid-June at water temperatures of 67–70°F (21°C).

# Shortnose gar
*Lepisosteus platostomus*                               32in (81cm)

**Identification** Olive-green fish with a moderately short, broad snout.
Width at nostrils into its length 4.6–7.1 times. Teeth in single row.
Body without spots. Abbreviate-heterocercal tail. Lateral line scales
60–64. Scales in a diagonal row 20–23.
**Habitat** Large rivers in current over a sandy bottom.
**Range** Mississippi River system.
**Comments** Feeds primarily on fish, but adults also regularly consume
crayfish and insects. Spawns from May-July at temperatures of
66–74°F (19–24°C) in shallow backwaters. Eggs scattered over
vegetation or other submerged objects.

# Bowfins – Amiidae

The bowfin family, Amiidae, contains only one species *(Amia calva)*. Bowfins have cycloid scales, an abbreviate-heterocercal tail, long dorsal fin, and a primitive skeleton, partly bone and partly cartilage. A gular plate occurs between the lower jaws.

## Bowfin
*Amia calva*                                                    34in (86cm)

**Identification** Abbreviate-heterocercal tail, long, low dorsal fin. Gular plate. Cycloid scales. Nostrils tubular. Caudal fin rounded with black spot in upper base.
**Habitat** Primarily a lowland species, inhabiting oxbow lakes, bayous, and swamps.
**Range** St Lawrence and Ottowa rivers west to Great Lakes, Mississippi River system; Minnesota south to Texas and Florida.
**Comments** Spawns from early April into June. Feeds on fishes and crayfishes. Caught by anglers on natural baits and occasionally artificial lures. Weighs around 4lbs (1.8kg).

# Freshwater Eels – Anguillidae

All freshwater eels in North America belong to a single species, the American eel, *Anguilla rostrata*. Eels superficially resemble lampreys, but differ in having well-developed jaws, minute imbedded cycloid scales, and pectoral fins. Freshwater eels are catadromous with adults spawning in the Atlantic Ocean near Bermuda before dying. Eggs hatch into *leptocephalus* larvae which find their way back to the mainland where they transform into the elver stage and migrate upstream.

## American eel
*Anguilla rostrata*                                          30in (76cm)

**Identification** Snake-like; no pelvic fins. Dorsal, caudal, and anal fins continuous. Well-developed jaws, two nostrils and paired pectoral fins. Small, embedded scales present. 3lbs (1.4kg) or under in weight.
**Habitat** Large to moderately large streams and rivers.
**Range** Atlantic and Gulf slopes of North America.
**Comments** Eels undergo one of the strangest migration odysseys of any fish species. After several years of living in fresh water, adults migrate downstream to salt water and then, by way of the Gulf Stream, to breeding grounds south of Bermuda to spawn and die. Eggs hatch into *leptocephalus* larvae which drift with the Gulf Stream toward North America and eventually find their way into freshwater streams.

# Mooneyes – Hiodontidae

Mooneyes and goldeyes are the only two species in this Family and are generally silvery, slab-sided fishes with large forward placed eyes, rounded snouts, cycloid scales, adipose eyelids, axillary processes, scaleless head, complete lateral lines, moderately long anal fins, and well-developed forked caudal fins.

## Goldeye
*Hiodon alosoides*                                                 20in (51cm)

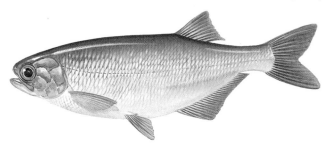

**Identification** Silvery; large mouth with well-developed canine teeth on jaws and tongue; large yellowish eye. A fleshy keel on midline of body. Dorsal fin origin situated behind the origin of the anal fin. Size around 3lbs (1.4kg).
**Habitat** Medium-sized to large rivers, but also in reservoirs.
**Range** Mississippi River system from Louisiana north to Great Plains and northwestern Canada almost to mouth of Mackenzie River, Northwest Territories.
**Comments** Primarily a nocturnal species, the large eyes are adapted to dim light conditions and to turbid habitats. Feeds on fish and both terrestrial and aquatic insects.

# Mooneye
*Hiodon tergisus*                                          11–15in (28–38cm)

**Identification** Greenish. Dorsal fin origin slightly in front of anal origin; fleshy keel; eye large and silvery. Weighs 12ozs–2lbs (0.3–0.9kg).

**Habitat** Large, clear streams, rivers, and lakes and seems to be less tolerant of turbid waters than the goldeye.

**Range** Mobile Bay basin west to Mississippi River basin, north through Mississippi River system (except Great Plains), north into Hudson Bay basin of south-central Canada.

**Comments** Feeds on aquatic macroinvertebrates and small fish under low light conditions at night or near dusk. Spawns in March, April and May in tributary streams over swift gravel shoals.

# Herrings – Clupeidae

Herrings are a large family (about 200 species) of mostly silvery, slab-sided, schooling fishes of worldwide distribution with many marine, several freshwater, and some anadromous species. In spite of their generally small size, many are valuable food fishes. Clupeids are characterized by a ventral keel having sharp, saw-toothed projections, no adipose fin, no lateral line, cycloid scales, naked heads, adipose eyelids, and small, flap-like projections (axillary processes) at the upper margins of the pectoral and pelvic fin bases. Caudal fin is deeply forked.

## Alabama shad
*Alosa alabamae*                                                18in (46cm)

**Identification** Silvery fish with large terminal mouth, no lateral line, and last ray of dorsal fin lacking an elongated slender filament. Upper and lower jaws almost equal in length. Tongue with a single median row of small teeth. Anal rays 18 or fewer. Gill rakers on lower limb of first arch more than 40.
**Habitat** Large to medium-sized rivers.
**Range** Gulf Coast rivers from Florida west to Louisiana; ascends rivers of Mississippi River system north to Illinois, Missouri, and Tennessee.
**Comments** Anadromous; adults spend most of their lives in the ocean returning to fresh water to spawn.

# Skipjack herring
*Alosa chrysochloris*

14in (36cm)

**Identification** Silvery; large terminal mouth reaching below the eye; deeply forked tail. Lower jaw projects beyond upper; black pigment confined to tip of jaw. Jaw teeth present; teeth on tongue in 2–4 rows; anal rays 17–19. Lateral line absent; scales in lateral series 53–60. Longitudinal row of small dark spots often dorsolaterally.
**Habitat** Prefers clear, open waters, often in swift current.
**Range** Western Florida to eastern Texas north in Mississippi River system to Minnesota and South Dakota.
**Comments** This migratory species reproduces over a prolonged period from March-July. Adults and juveniles feed primarily on fish. Lives four years.

# Alewife
*Alosa pseudoharengus*

15in (38cm)

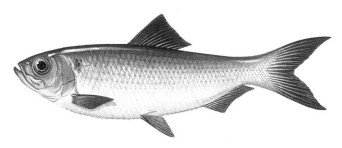

**Identification** Small, silvery fish with large eye, well-developed adipose eyelid, and oblique mouth. Humeral spot present. Lower jaw extending beyond upper jaw. Tongue with patch of teeth. Last dorsal ray not elongate. Lateral series 42–50. Well-developed ventral scutes.
**Habitat** Estuarine environments; entering fresh water in lakes and streams.
**Range** Great Lakes; Newfoundland to South Carolina.

# American shad
*Alosa sapidissima*

30in (76cm)

**Identification** Deep-bodied, elongate shad with a small eye, adipose eyelid and rounded dorsal and ventral profile. Large black humeral spot followed by several (4–27) smaller, dark spots. Last ray of dorsal fin not elongate. Gill rakers 59–73.
**Habitat** Estuarine habitats and fresh water.
**Range** Atlantic Coast from Newfoundland to Florida.

# Gizzard shad
*Dorosoma cepedianum*

20in (51 cm)

**Identification** Silvery, slab-sided, with blunt snout. Upper jaw projects beyond lower. Adipose eyelid present. Large dark humeral spot. Last ray of dorsal fin elongated into a thin filament. Anal fin rays 29–35. Caudal fin forked. Maximum weight 3.5lbs (1.6kg)
**Habitat** Pelagic schooling species in the open waters.
**Range** Great Lakes and St Lawrence River to South Dakota and central Minnesota south to New Mexico and east to Gulf of Mexico extending up Atlantic Coast to New York.
**Comments** Stocked in man-made reservoirs where young provide food for most native gamefishes. Feeds on zooplankton, phyto-plankton and microcrustaceans.

# Threadfin shad
*Dorosoma petenense*

8in (20cm)

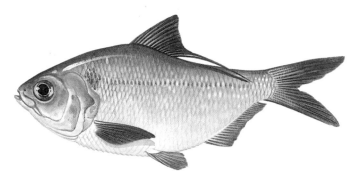

**Identification** Silvery; deeply compressed body; upper jaw not projecting beyond lower jaw. Small dark humeral spot. Last ray of dorsal fin elongated into a thin filament. Anal fin rays 20–27.
**Habitat** Lakes, reservoirs, large rivers.
**Range** Florida west to Texas, north in Mississippi River system, north to Missouri and Ohio River system of Kentucky.
**Comments** Forage fish stocked in reservoirs. This pelagic schooling species has been widely stocked in reservoirs from Virginia to California. Feeds on plankton.

# Trouts – Salmonidae

The trout family is a widely distributed, relatively small, family (around 70 species) occurring in North America, Europe, and Asia. Found in both fresh water and marine environments, these cold-water fishes are of great economic significance. They are important game fishes, and some (salmon, whitefish, and graylings) are of commercial importance in northern North America. Salmonids have a fleshy adipose fin, tiny cycloid scales on the body with more than 70 scales in the lateral line, fins are soft-rayed, an axillary process is present at the pelvic fin origin, and a large mouth.

## Cisco

*Coregonus artedii*                                    12in (30cm)

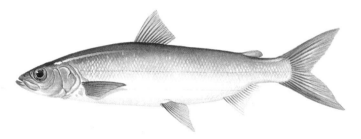

**Identification** Silvery with a terminal mouth (lower jaw projecting slightly beyond upper jaw), adipose fin, and forked tail. Dorsal fin rays 10–15; anal rays 11–15. Pelvic axillary process. Lateral line scales 63–94, Gill rakers 43–52.
**Habitat** Lakes.
**Range** North-central and eastern United States and most of Canada.
**Comments** The cisco is the most variable and wide-ranging species within this group.

# Lake whitefish
*Coregonus clupeaformis*                                    24in (61cm)

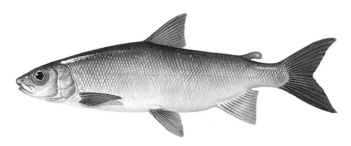

**Identification** Slender, silvery fish with a short head, inferior mouth overhung by snout, adipose fin, and forked caudal fin. Double flap of skin between nostrils. Gill rakers 19–33. Tongue with teeth; jaws without teeth. Anal rays 10–14. Lateral line with 70–97 scales.
**Habitat** Big riverine environments and lakes.
**Range** Atlantic coastal drainages westward across Canada and the northern USA to British Colombia. Yukon Territory and Alaska.
**Comments** Most important commercial freshwater fish in Canada. Unfortunately, environmental deterioration and depletion of stocks have combined to reduce commercial yields in recent years.

# Golden trout
*Oncorhynchus aguabonita*                                   12in (30cm)

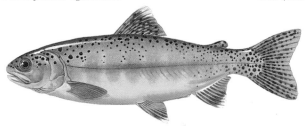

**Identification** Bright red to red-orange belly and cheeks, lower sides golden, lateral band red-orange, and deep olive-green back. Sides with 10 parr marks centered on lateral line. Dorsal and caudal fins with large spots. Spots scattered across back and upper sides. Pectoral fin orange; pelvic and anal fins orange with whitish tips preceded by a black band. Dorsal fin with white or orangish tip. Lateral line with 175–210 scales. Gill rakers 17–21. Adipose fin.
**Habitat** Clear, cold streams and lakes above 6890ft (2100m).
**Range** Upper Kern River basin, California; introduced in western states.

# Apache trout
*Oncorhynchus apache*                                    18in (46cm)

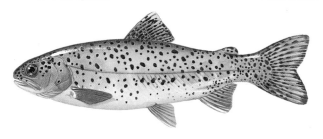

**Identification** Beautiful fish with an adipose fin, large dark spot
behind the eye, and yellow to golden sides. Head, dorsum, sides, and
fins dark-spotted. Dorsal, pelvic and anal fins white-tipped. Underside
of head orange to yellowish-orange. Lateral line complete with
112–124 scales.
**Habitat** Riffles and pools of cool, clear mountain streams above
7544ft (2300m).
**Range** Little Colorado and Salt River headwaters; East Central
Arizona.

# Cutthroat trout
*Oncorhynchus clarki*                                    30in (76cm)

**Identification** Bright reddish-orange dash (cut-throat mark) present
on each side of the throat. Teeth well developed on jaws, tongue, and
palatine bones; tongue with two rows of teeth. Lateral line complete
with 150–230 scales. Scales cycloid. Maximum size 41lbs (18.6kg).
**Habitat** Lakes, mountain streams, and estuaries.
**Range** Alaska south to California, east to Colorado; British Columbia
and Alberta south to New Mexico. Introduced elsewhere.

# Coho Salmon
*Oncorhynchus kisutch*　　　　　　　　　　　　　　39in (1m)

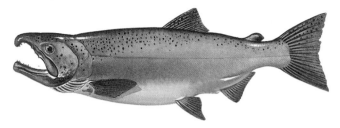

**Identification** Streamlined. Adipose fin; large mouth. Teeth on jaws, head and shaft of vomer, palatines and tongue. Dorsum with small dark spots. Caudal fin with rough striations on fin rays and black dots on upper lobe. Gum area at base of teeth of lower jaw pale. Pyloric caeca 45–80. Gill rakers 19–25. Lateral line scales small, 212–148.
**Habitat** Coastal streams.
**Range** Pacific Ocean and its tributary drainages: Alaska to southern California. Introduced in the Great Lakes.
**Comments** Valuable commercial and sport fish. Anadromous species, returning to fresh water to spawn in the fall of the year. Adults die after spawning is completed.

# Rainbow trout
*Oncorhynchus mykiss*　　　　　　　　　　　　　　45in (1.1m)

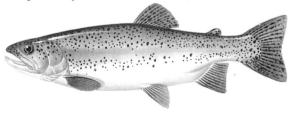

**Identification** Teeth absent on rear of tongue. Adipose fin present. Dorsum and upper sides olive green, thickly speckled with black spots. Dorsal, adipose, and caudal fins spotted. Pinkish to reddish band on sides. Lateral line scales 100–150. Gill rakers 16–22.
**Habitat** Clear, upland stream pools; below reservoirs in cold water.
**Range** Originally native to Pacific Coast from Alaska south to northern Mexico. Introduced into suitable habitats in Canada, and eastern United States.
**Comments** This trout is highly variable over its native range. Much confusion continues over the designation of taxonomic rank for previously, described races, varieties and sub-species. On the Pacific Coast it is anadromous and called the "steelhead."

# Sockeye salmon
*Oncorhynchus nerka*

33in (84cm)

**Identification** Adipose fin; premaxillaries not protractile. Body color in freshwater breeding males bright red with a greenish-olive head and black snout; females with grayish-red color and yellow blotches. Gill rakers 28–40 on first arch. Pyloric caeca 45–115. Lateral line scales 120–150.
**Habitat** In fresh water, clear, cool streams, rivers, and lakes; open ocean,
**Range** Pacific Coast; Alaska to California. Stocked elsewhere in northern lakes.
**Comments** The sockeye salmon is an anadromous species spawning in the fall in 1–30ft (30cm–9m) at 41–51°F (5–10°C). Males develop prolonged, hooked, upturned snout, and a gaping mouth and small hump anterior to the dorsal fin.

# Chinook salmon
*Oncorhynchus tshawytscha*

58in (1.5m)

**Identification** Adipose fin. Smooth striations on the caudal fin rays, black gums at base of teeth. Dorsum and caudal fin with black spots. Teeth on both jaws, head and shaft of vomer, palatines and tongue. Gill rakers 16–26 on first arch. Lateral line scales small 130–165. Maximum size up to 126lbs (57.2kg).
**Habitat** Large rivers in fresh water, mid-depths and surface of ocean.
**Range** Pacific Coast; Alaska to southern California. Introduced widely.

# Round whitefish
*Prosopium cylindraceum*                                22in (56cm)

**Identification** A cylindrical silvery fish with a single flap of skin between nostrils, small ventral, mouth overhung by snout, adipose fin, and forked caudal fin. Scales outlined with dark pigment on back. Gill rakers 14–21. Tongue with teeth; jaws without teeth. Lateral line scales 74–108 scales.
**Habitat** Deep lakes; large streams.
**Range** Alaska, Canada, south to Great Lakes and New England.

# Mountain whitefish
*Prosopium williamsoni*                                 12in (30cm)

**Identification** Silvery; single flap of skin between the nostrils and an adipose fin. Mouth small and ventral, overhung by snout. Gill rakers 19–26. Pelvic axillary process present. Sides outlined in black pigment. Lateral line complete with 74–90 scales.
**Habitat** Lakes and streams.
**Range** Western North America from Nevada north through Montana, Wyoming, and Idaho to Alberta and British Columbia to the Yukon-British Columbia border.

# Atlantic salmon
*Salmo salar*                                    53in (1.3m)

**Identification** Adipose fin, slightly forked caudal fin. Many small dark spots on head, body and dorsal fin. Gill cover with two or three large spots. Males with red spots on sides. Breeding males with lower jaw hooked upward. Gill rakers 15–20. Usually 12 branchiostegals. Vomerine teeth not well developed. Scales cycloid. Lateral line scales 109–121.
**Habitat** Freshwater streams and lakes; coastal waters.
**Range** North Atlantic and coastal drainages from Arctic Circle, Quebec south to Delaware River; Lake Ontario. Landlocked populations present in several New England states.
**Comments** A highly prized game fish, the Atlantic salmon is an anadromous species ascending mountain streams in the fall to spawn over gravel pools. Maximum size of 79lb 2oz (33.9kg).

# Brown trout
*Salmo trutta*                                    40in (1m)

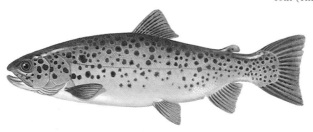

**Identification** An olive-brown, streamlined fish with scattered red or orange spots having blue halos. Dorsal and adipose fins with black spots. Dark spots absent in caudal fin. Teeth absent on midline of tongue. Lateral line scales 120–140. Gill rakers 14–17. Weighs up to 33lb 10oz (15kg).
**Habitat** Moderate to high gradient streams and rivers.
**Range** Not native to North America; widely stocked throughout much of Canada and USA.
**Comments** This introduced trout (native to Europe and Asia) is a favorite among anglers. It spawns in fall and early winter at 55–57°F (12–13°C). Adults eat mainly crayfish and fish.

# Arctic char
*Salvelinus alpinus*

18in (46cm)

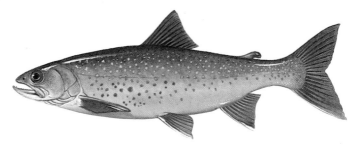

**Identification** Terete fish with a rounded snout, large terminal mouth, 23–32 gill rakers, 37–75 pyloric caeca, and pink to red spots on sides and back, largest of which are generally larger than pupil of eye.
**Habitat** Inshore marine waters, lakes and rivers.
**Range** Circumpolar, from Aleutian Islands, Alaska Peninsula and Kodiak Island north to Arctic Ocean; south to New England.
**Comments** The Arctic char has the most northerly distribution of any freshwater fish.

# Brook trout
*Salvelinus fontinalis*

21in (53cm)

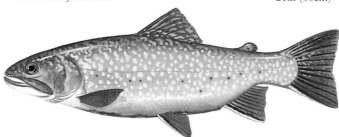

**Identification** Body color olive-green on back with worm-like markings. Sides lighter with red spots within blue halos. Undersides orange or reddish in adult breeding males. Anterior rays of pectoral, pelvic, and anal fins milky white followed by a black stripe; posterior parts of those fins orange. Maximum size 14lb 8oz (6.6kg).
**Habitat** Cold, clear streams.
**Range** Native to eastern Canada and eastern USA and Great Lakes region south through Appalachians to Georgia.
**Comments** This beautiful trout is pursued by anglers in some of the smallest streams. It prefers cover such as rocks, logs and undercut banks. Spawns in late fall and winter at 55°F (12°C) in gradual riffles.

# Dolly Varden
*Salvelinus malma* 18in (46cm)

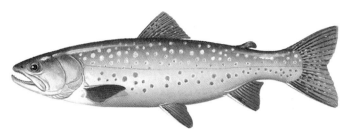

**Identification** An elongate salmonid with a moderately long head, rounded snout, no worm-like markings on its back, pink or red spots on sides present, gill rakers 11–26, and 13–35 pyloric caeca. Lateral line scales 105–142. Maximum size 31lb 8oz (14.5kg).
**Habitat** Both anadromous and non-anadromous populations exist in clear freshwater streams.
**Range** From Arctic coast or Alaska south through British Columbia to Montana, Nevada, and Idaho and northern California.


# Lake trout
*Salvelinus namaycush* 50in (1.3m)

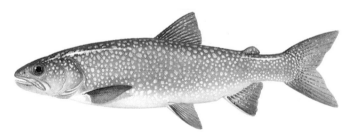

**Identification** Gray to greenish-brown trout with dorsum, sides, head, adipose fin and median fins with many vermiculations and small creamy spots. Pectoral, pelvic, and anal fins often orange with whitish margin. Pyloric caeca 95–170. Lateral line 185–210 scales. Caudal fin deeply forked.
**Habitat** Occurs in deep, cold lakes and rivers.
**Range** Alaska, Canada and Great Lakes region, eastward to New York and Maine.
**Comments** Largest native trout in North America, attaining a length of over 4ft (1.2m). Foods range from plankton and insects to fishes. Spawns at night from September in the north to June in the south over boulder or rubble bottoms in inland lakes at 48–55°F (9°C–13°C) in the southern part of range.

## Inconnu (sheefish)
*Stenodus leucichthys*                                    30in (76cm)

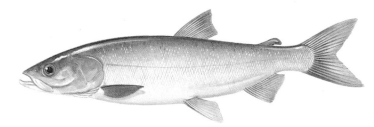

**Identification** Silvery fish with lower jaw protruding beyond upper
jaw, adipose fin, axillary process at base of pelvic fin, and only 13–17
gill rakers on lower limb of first gill arch. Dorsal fin high and pointed
with 11–19 rays. Caudal fin forked.
**Habitat** Large and cold rivers and lakes.
**Range** Alaska; Canada in Mackenzie drainage and east to Anderson
River.

## Arctic grayling
*Thymallus arcticus*                                      30in (76cm)

**Identification** Bluish-black to purplish fish with long dorsal fin
(17–25 rays), elongate body, adipose fin, and deeply forked caudal fin.
Sides with numerous diamond-shaped spots anteriorly and a dark
stripe from pectoral to pelvic fins.
**Habitat** Cold, clear streams, rivers and lakes.
**Range** From Alaska east through Canada to Hudson Bay south to
Montana and the Great Lakes. Transplanted in western USA.

# Smelts – Osmeridae

Smelts are north circumpolar in distribution, occurring in marine and freshwater habitats in North America, Europe, and Asia. Nine species occur in North America. Smelts are important commercial and sport fishes characterized by a terminal mouth, forked tail, adipose fin, body with small easily shed cycloid scales, and gill membranes not joined across throat.

## Rainbow smelt
*Osmerus mordax*                                    13in (33m)

**Identification** Silvery fish with teeth on tongue and jaws. Roof of mouth with one to three large canine teeth on each side of the vomer. Adipose fin present. Caudal fin deeply forked. Lateral line incomplete.
**Habitat** Although most populations are anadromous and ascend freshwater streams to spawn. Landlocked populations do exist which are strictly freshwater. Freshwater populations inhabit large rivers.
**Range** Labrador south to North Virginia, coastal areas of Alaska, introduced in Great Lakes and Mississippi River south to Louisiana.
**Comments** Spawning occurs in the spring when water temperatures exceed 45°F (4°C) at night in shallow water over a gravel bottom.

# Longfin smelt
*Spirinchus thaleichthys*

6in (15cm)

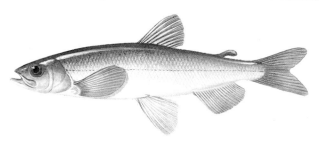

**Identification** Slender fish with a short head, long upper jaw reaching to below the middle of the eye, the fine teeth in a single row on the vomer and palatine bone, large eye, and 38–47 gill rakers on first arch. Dorsal fin with 8–10 rays. Anal fin rays 15–19,
**Habitat** Anadromous; enters fresh water to spawn. A few landlocked populations are known.
**Range** Pacific Coast from San Francisco Bay to Prince William Sound, Alaska.

# Eulachon
*Thaleichthys pacificus*

8in (20cm)

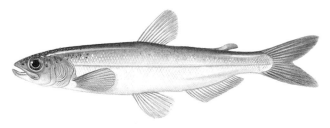

**Identification** A slender fish with an adipose fin, short head, long snout, small eye, and large oblique mouth (lower jaw extending past upper jaw). Vomer bone with large canine teeth. Dorsal fin rays 10–13. Anal fin rays 18–23. Lateral line complete with 70–78 scales. Caudal fin forked.
**Habitat** Anadromous; lives in ocean but returns to fresh water to spawn.
**Range** Pacific Coast from California to Alaska.

# Mudminnows – Umbridae

The mudminnows represent a rather small family containing only five species characterized by soft-rayed fins, abdominal pelvics, rounded caudal fin, and cycloid scales.

## Central mudminnow
*Umbra limi*                                                    5in (13cm)

**Identification** Sides with 10–14 indistinct bars. Caudal fin base with a prominent dusky ventral bar. Caudal fin rounded. Lateral line absent; scales in series 34–37.
**Habitat** Heavily vegetated sloughs, ditches, bogs and swamps over mud substrates.
**Range** Southern Canada and central USA.
**Comments** Tolerant of waters with low dissolved oxygen and acid waters. Spawns in April at 55–60°F (12.8–15.6°C) in flooded marginal reaches.

## Alaska blackfish .
*Dallia pectoralis*                                             7in (18cm)

**Identification** Brown cylindrical fish with a short flattened head, small eye, short snout, large, rounded pectoral fins, and four to six bars or blotches on sides. 76–100 in lateral series.
**Habitat** Sluggish, weed-choked streams, ponds, swamps and lakes.
**Range** Alaska and Bering Sea Islands.

# Pikes – Esocidae

The pike family has four North American species easily recognizable by the distinctive "duck's bill" shape of the snout. The mouth is large, with many sharp teeth, and the single dorsal fin is far back on the body. The caudal fin is forked, the body is covered with cycloid scales.

## Grass pickerel
*Esox americanus*                                    14in (36cm)

**Identification** Snout formed like a duck's bill; large mouth with sharp canine teeth. Sides with bars and vermiculations. Dark vertical bar extends down from eye. Four sensory pores on lower jaw. Branchiostegal rays 11 or 12. Cheek and opercle fully scaled.
**Habitat** Quiet, heavily vegetated backwaters of small streams, bayous, swamps and sloughs.
**Range** Mississippi River basin, Gulf of Mexico drainages, Atlantic Coastal Plain south to Quebec.
**Comments** One of the smallest members of the family. Late fall, early winter or spring spawner at 40–53°F (4–11°C). Lives eight years in Canada.

# Northern pike
*Esox lucius*                                        52in (1.3m)

**Identification** Snout shaped like a duck's bill. Dorsal and anal fins set far back on body. Sides with numerous small, oval white or yellow spots. Lower jaw with five sensory pores on each side. Cheek fully scaled; upper half of operculum scaled. May reach 40lbs (18kg).
**Habitat** Cold lakes, reservoirs, and rivers with little current and dense aquatic vegetation.
**Range** Holarctic from Alaska throughout Canada south to Missouri; east to Pennsylvania and New York.
**Comments** The northern pike has the greatest tolerance for cold environments of any esocid. Widely sought by anglers as a sport fish. Considered to be the most widely distributed freshwater fish in the world. Feeds almost entirely on fishes and other vertebrates. May live up to 24 years.

# Muskellunge
*Esox masquinongy*                                   6ft (1.8m)

**Identification** Snout shaped like a duck's bill. Dorsal and anal fins placed far back on body. Cheek and operculum scaled only on upper half. Branchiostegal rays 17–19. Lower jaw with six to nine sensory pores on each side. Lateral line complete with 130–157 scales.
**Habitat** Lakes, reservoirs and backwaters of rivers with thick vegetation.
**Range** Quebec and Ontario south to Tennessee; from St Lawrence River to North Georgia.
**Comments** The muskellunge is the largest species in the family. It is highly sought by anglers as it can weigh up to 70lbs (31.7kg). It consumes primarily fishes, but may eat small ducks and muskrats. Spawns in the spring at 48–59°F (9–15°C). Lives up to 25 years.

# Chain pickerel
*Esox niger*

31in (79cm)

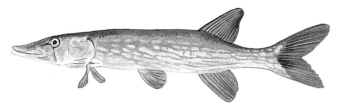

**Identification** Dark chain-like markings on sides. Dark bar under eye. Snout shaped like a duck's bill. Lower jaw with a row of four sensory pores on each side. Cheek and opercle fully scaled. Can weigh up to 9lbs (4kg).

**Habitat** Streams, lakes, swamps with vegetation.

**Range** Mississippi River system north to Missouri and Kentucky; Gulf of Mexico drainages; Atlantic Coastal Plain north to Nova Scotia, New Brunswick, and Quebec.

**Comments** The chain pickerel spawns from late winter to spring at 46–51°F (8–11°C) over vegetation. Adults feed on fish and other vertebrates.

# Characins – Characidae

This large family (300 species) occurs primarily in Africa and
South America. Although members resemble minnows
(Cyprinidae), all characins possess an adipose fin. Only one
species, the Mexican tetra, ranges into southwestern USA.

## Mexican tetra
*Astyanax mexicanus*                               5in (13cm)

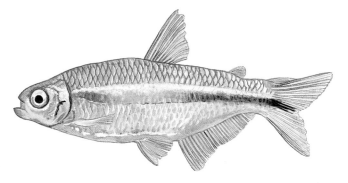

**Identification**  Small deep-bodied fish with a deeply forked tail and
well-developed adipose fin. Conspicuous black lateral band. Head
short; jaws have multicuspid teeth.
**Habitat**  Rivers and creeks with slow to moderate current.
**Range**  South Texas and New Mexico south to South America;
widely introduced in other areas including Texas, New Mexico,
Arizona and California.
**Comments**  Most northern representative of the Characidae.
Occasionally seen in aquarium shops. Introduced widely.

# Carps and Minnows – Cyprinidae

The family Cyprinidae is the largest and most widely distributed family of modern fishes with about 1500 species worldwide. Over 280 species inhabit North America. While most minnows are small, several species reach lengths of 3–5ft (1.4–1.5m). Members are characterized by the presence of a Weberian apparatus, pharyngeal teeth, toothless, cycloid scales and adipose fin absent.

## Chiselmouth
*Acrocheilus alutaceus*                                          12in (30cm)

**Identification** Forked caudal fin. Upper jaw with fleshy lip and small straight, cartilaginous plate. Lower jaw with hard cartilaginous sheath with straight cutting edge. Intestine twice body length. Lateral line scales 85–93. Pharyngeal teeth 5–4 or 5–5.
**Habitat** Streams, rivers and lakes with firm bottom.
**Range** British Columbia south to Oregon, Idaho, and Nevada.

# Central stoneroller
*Campostoma anomalum*                                    8in (20cm)

**Identification** Mouth inferior; lower jaw with a cartilaginous ridge.
Randomly scattered dark flecks on sides. Lateral line scales 49–57.
**Habitat** Clear streams with gravel, rubble or bedrock substrates and
moderate to swift current.
**Range** Southern Ontario, south through most of eastern USA, west
to Rockies except for southern Atlantic coastal states.

# Goldfish
*Carassius auratus*                                      16in (40cm)

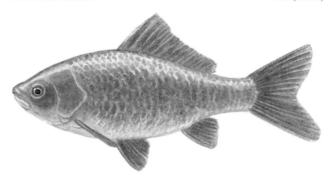

**Identification** Gold, orange, and whitish varieties exist. Dorsal fin
long (18–19 rays) with one hard serrated spine. Barbels absent.
Lateral line scales 26–30. Anal fin with one hard serrated spine, 5–7
rays. May weigh up to 2lb 8oz (1kg).
**Habitat** Ponds and lakes with a soft substrate and generally aquatic
vegetation.
**Range** Introduced in warmer waters of USA, Canada and Mexico.
**Comments** The goldfish is a native of China. Due to its popularity in
the aquarium trade, many state records are releases of aquarium
inhabitants.

# Rosyside dace
*Clinostomus funduloides* 4in (10cm)

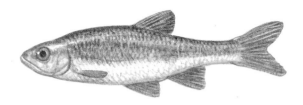

**Identification** Streamlined; extremely large terminal mouth (lower jaw extending beyond upper). No barbels. Sides with dusky mid-lateral stripe and numerous, scattered dark scales. Lateral line decurved, complete with 48–57 scales.
**Habitat** Small, clear gravel and rock-bottomed streams with moderate current.
**Range** New Jersey, Pennsylvania south to Georgia, west to Tennessee, Mississippi, Kentucky and Ohio.

# Lake chub
*Couesius plumbeus* 4in (10cm)

**Identification** Barbeled minnow (barbels not terminal), with a slender peduncle, short head and bluntly rounded snout. Body with specialized darkened scales. Lateral line complete with 54–65 scales. Pharyngeal teeth generally 2, 4–4, 2. Pelvic axillary scale weakly developed, no fleshy stays on dorsal aspect of pelvic fins.
**Habitat** Streams, rivers and lakes.
**Range** Occurs throughout Canada to northern USA, south to Iowa, Colorado, and Idaho.

# Grass carp
*Ctenopharyngodon idella*

39in (1m)

**Identification** Elongate, stout-bodied, blunt-headed fish with a terminal, non-protractile mouth with thin lips, no barbels, and anal fin situated far posteriorly. Intestine long with several loops. Pharyngeal teeth in principal row with deep parallel grooves. Maximum size up to 100lbs (45.4kg).
**Habitat** Rivers, but stocked in impoundments.
**Range** Widely introduced into more than 35 states.
**Comments** Native of China. Introduced into Arkansas in 1963 in ponds for aquatic weed control. By 1990s this species had escaped into surrounding waterways and was being caught by commercial fishermen. Although it is supposed to eat only vegetation, it has proven an extremely controversial species with several states barring its stocking.


# Satinfin shiner
*Cyprinella analostana*

3½in (9cm)

**Identification** Silvery-blue shiner with a pointed snout, terminal mouth, small eye and no basicaudal spot. Scales dark-edged giving a diamond-shaped appearance. Posterior membranes of dorsal fin pigmented. Pectoral rays 13–14. Anal rays 9. Lateral line scales 35–37. Phayngeal teeth 1, 4–4, 1.
**Habitat** Small to large streams with slow to moderate current over sand or gravel substrates.
**Range** Lake Ontario drainage, New York, New York south to North Carolina in Atlantic coast drainage.

# Bluntface shiner
*Cyprinella camura*                                    4½in (11cm)

**Identification**  A deep-bodied shiner with a blunt snout, small eye
and oblique mouth. Whitish bar at base of caudal fin flaring dorsally
and ventrally. Black blotches on posterior membranes of dorsal fin.
Anal rays 9. Lateral line scales 36–41.
**Habitat**  Swift, clear upland streams over gravel bottoms.
**Range**  Arkansas and lower Mississippi River system from Oklahoma
and Kansas to Mississippi and Tennessee.


# Whitetail shiner
*Cyprinella galactura*                                 5in (13cm)

**Identification**  Silvery, slab-sided shiner with two conspicuous white
patches at base of caudal fin. Anal rays 9. Pharyngeal teeth 1, 4–4, 1.
Lateral line scales 39–41. Posterior ray membranes of dorsal black.
**Habitat**  Medium to large, clear, high gradient streams with silt-free
gravel or rock substrates.
**Range**  Southern Missouri and northern Arkansas; Tennessee and
Cumberland drainages of Alabama, Georgia, North Carolina,
Tennessee, Virginia, and Kentucky.

# Red shiner
*Cyprinella lutrensis*    3in (7.6cm)

**Identification** Sides steel-blue with diamond-shaped scales outlined in black on dorsum and sides. Dark wedge-shaped bar located just posterior to opercle. Dorsal fin without intensive black pigment on the posterior membranes. Anal fin rays 9. Lateral line scales 32–37.
**Habitat** Sluggish streams and large rivers, slow to moderate current over sand or gravel substrates.
**Range** West of the Mississippi River from Wyoming and Minnesota, south to Texas; introduced widely elsewhere.
Comments The red shiner is the most common and abundant inhabitant of the Plains Region. This important forage and bait fish has recently become a popular aquarium fish, marketed under the name "African Fire Barb."

# Spotfin chub
*Cyprinella monacha*    3½in (9cm)

**Identification** Barbeled minnow with silvery to steel-blue sides. Eyes small. Snout extending beyond upper lip. Dorsal fin rays with dark spot on posterior rays. Large, black caudal spot present. Lateral line scales 52–62.
**Habitat** Moderate to swift sections of large, clear streams over gravel or rock substrates.
**Range** Tennessee River drainage; Virginia south to Georgia and Alabama.

# Spotfin shiner
*Cyprinella spiloptera*                                    4in (10cm)

**Identification** Scales diamond-shaped. Dark lateral band on caudal
peduncle narrow and little above midline. Anal rays 8. Pharyngeal
teeth 1, 4–4, 1. Dorsal fin with last two or three membranes blackish.
**Habitat** Medium to large-sized streams and small rivers in pools with
gravel or sandy substrates, primarily in moderate currents.
**Range** St Lawrence River and Great Lakes drainage in Quebec and
Ontario; from New York to the Dakotas in the north and Alabama to
Oklahoma in the south.

# Steelcolor shiner
*Cyprinella whipplei*                                    4½in (11cm)

**Identification** Slab-sided shiner. No basicaudal spot. Last two to
three membranes of dorsal fin with black pigment. Anal rays 9.
Pharyngeal teeth 1, 4–4, 1.
**Habitat** Medium to large-sized clear streams with gravel bottoms.
**Range** Ohio through the lower Mississippi basin to Louisiana.

# Blacktail shiner
*Cyprinella venusta*                                    5in (13cm)

**Identification** Slab-sided shiner with a large, black basicaudal spot. Large, diamond-shaped scales outlined in black. Anal rays 8. Pharyngeal teeth 1, 4–4, 1. Posterior three dorsal fin ray membranes are blackened.
**Habitat** Medium to large streams and rivers, sluggish ditches, and oxbow lakes over sand bottoms.
**Range** Southern USA from Texas and Oklahoma north to Missouri and Illinois and east to Georgia and Florida.


# Common carp
*Cyprinus carpio*                                    30in (76cm)

**Identification** Long dorsal fin 18-21 rays. Two pairs of barbels on upper lip. Dorsal fin with one hard serrated spine. Anal fin also with a hard serrated spine and 5–6 rays. Lateral line scales 32–37.
**Habitat** Prefers quiet, shallow waters of rivers and impoundments in turbid or clear water over mud or silt with aquatic vegetation.
**Range** Introduced throughout the USA, southern Canada and Mexico.
**Comments** This Asian fish was first introduced into the USA in late 1877 by the United States Fish Commission as a food fish. It can survive almost anywhere it can find suitable food. Although popular as a food fish in Europe, carp have never proved popular in North America as food or game fishes.

# Streamline chub
*Erimystax dissimilis*                    4½in (11cm)

**Identification** Large-eyed, barbeled minnow. Snout projecting beyond small, horizontal mouth. Series of six to nine dark roundish blotches laterally. Anal rays 7. Pharyngeal teeth 4–4.
**Habitat** Large, clear swift streams and rivers over clean gravel or rock bottoms. Intolerant of turbidity and siltation.
**Range** Ohio River drainage from Alabama and Tennessee north to New York; east of Mississippi River in southern Missouri and northern Arkansas.

# Gravel chub
*Erimystax x-punctatus*                    4in (10cm)

**Identification** Barbeled minnow with conspicuous X-shaped markings over back and sides. Eye large, snout projecting beyond upper lip. Mouth inferior. Anal fin rays 7.
**Habitat** Swift, deep riffles and raceways in medium to large, clear, gravel-bottomed streams.
**Range** Ohio River basin east to Pennsylvania; Mississippi River system from Minnesota south to Arkansas and Oklahoma.

# Cutlips minnow
*Exoglossum maxillingua*                                    5in (13cm)

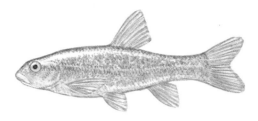

**Identification** Unique ventral mouth having a lower jaw of three
lobes (central lobe tongue-like, outer lobes fleshy). Barbels absent.
Lateral line complete with 50–53 scales. Anal rays 7. Pharyngeal teeth
1, 4–4, 1.
**Habitat** Small gravel and rock-bottomed streams and rivers in riffles
and pools.
**Range** Southern Canada south to North Carolina.

# Tui chub
*Gila bicolor*                                              14in (36cm)

**Identification** Robust minnow. Large head, small mouth, dusky
lateral band, decurved lateral line, stubby gill rakers, and often
developing a hump behind head. Lateral line scales 44–60. Anal rays
7–9, usually 8. Pharyngeal teeth 5–5, 5–4, or 4–4.
**Habitat** Weedy shallow lakes or quiet waters of sluggish rivers.
**Range** Owens and Mojave Rivers, Pit River, California. Interior
basins of Nevada and Oregon. Introduced in Oregon and Washington.

# Bonytail
*Gila elegans*

24in (61cm)

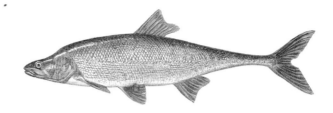

**Identification** Narrow caudal peduncle. Large falcate fins. Snout broadly rounded. Adults with distinctive hump on nape. Caudal fin deeply forked. Lateral line complete with 75–88 scales. Pharyngeal teeth 2, 5–4, 2.
**Habitat** Large, turbid rivers in swift channel reaches.
**Range** Colorado River system (Wyoming to Mexico). Currently in Green River drainage, Utah and Mohave Reservoir, Arizona/Nevada border.

# Roundtail chub
*Gila robusta*

17in (43cm)

**Identification** Flattened head, small eyes, terminal mouth. Slender caudal peduncle. Dorsal fin with 9–10 rays. Origin of dorsal fin posterior to pelvic fin insertion. Caudal fin deeply forked. Lateral line complete with 75–95 scales.
**Habitat** Large turbid streams, rivers and lakes.
**Range** Colorado River system (Wyoming, New Mexico).

# California roach
*Hesperoleucas symmetricus*                              4in (10cm)

**Identification** Dorsal fin rays 7–10, origin behind pelvic insertion. Predorsal scale rows 32–28. Anal rays 6–9. Lateral line with 47–63 scales. Pharyngeal teeth 5–4.
**Habitat** Small, intermittent tributaries to larger streams.
**Range** Pitt River drainage, southern Oregon; Sacramento and San Joaquin drainage system, central California.


# Brassy minnow
*Hybognathus hankinsoni*                                4in (10cm)

**Identification** Subterminal mouth; no barbels and snout rounded, slightly overhanging mouth. Dorsal fin rounded. Anal fin rays 8. Scale radii about 20 in adult. Pharyngeal teeth 4–4.
**Habitat** Small, sluggish, weedy creeks; also occurs in cool, acid waters of bog streams and lakes.
**Range** From Kansas northward to Canada, east to New York, west to Montana and southern Canada.

# Cypress minnow
*Hybognathus hayi*

3½in (9cm)

**Identification** Slab-sided minnow. Snout broadly rounded, barely visible from beneath. Diamond-shaping pattern of cross-hatching on dorso-lateral region. Predorsal scale rows 14–16.
**Habitat** Quiet backwater and oxbow lakes over mud and detritus bottoms.
**Range** Lower Mississippi basin from southern Illinois and southwestern Indiana south to Louisiana; west to Sabine River drainage, Texas, and east to Alabama along Gulf coast drainages

# Mississippi silvery minnow
*Hybognathus nuchalis*

7in (18cm)

**Identification** Dark mid-dorsal stripe present. Snout blunt, rounded and overhanging mouth. Eye diameter larger than width of mouth. Origin of dorsal fin anterior to pelvic fin insertion. Gut long and coiled; peritoneum black.
**Habitat** Clear pools and backwaters of large creeks and rivers with slow current.
**Range** Central Mississippi River system from Minnesota and Ohio south to Texas and Alabama.

## Plains minnow
*Hybognathus placitus*                                    5in (13cm)

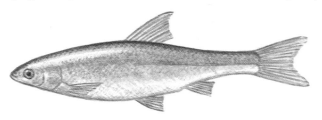

**Identification** Very small eye. Mid-dorsal stripe well developed.
Dorsal origin over pelvic insertion. Anal rays 8. Lateral line scales
36–39. Pharyngeal teeth 4–4.
**Habitat** Main channels of turbid, silt and sand-bottomed streams and
rivers.
**Range** Montana to North Dakota south to Texas.


## Striped shiner
*Luxilus chrysocephalus*                                  7in (19cm)

**Identification** Dark predorsal stripe. Broad dark lateral band, and
three dark horizontal lines running from behind upper head to mid-
dorsal stripe. Anal rays 9.
**Habitat** Small to moderate-sized streams with moderate current,
clear water and rocky, sandy or gravel bottoms.
**Range** Ontario, Canada; New York west to Wisconsin, south to
Alabama and west Missouri, Oklahoma and Texas.

# Warpaint shiner
*Luxilus coccogenis*                                    5in (13cm)

**Identification** Red upper lip, vertical red line posterior to eye, and
edge of operculum black. Base of dorsal fin reddish anteriorly, bluish
black posteriorly.
**Habitat** Clear, swift, medium to large gravel and rock-bottomed
streams.
**Range** Virginia south to Tennessee, South Carolina, Georgia west to
Alabama.

# Common shiner
*Luxilus cornutus*                                      6in (15cm)

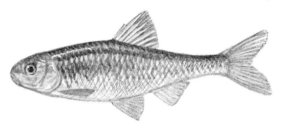

**Identification** Dark predorsal stripe present. Chin without dusky
pigment. Anal rays 8–9. Lateral line scales 36–44.
**Habitat** Clear streams and small rivers with moderate current in
pools with firm bottoms and gravel riffles.
**Range** Nova Scotia west to Saskatchewan, south to Virginia, and
west to Wyoming and Colorado.

# Duskystripe shiner
*Luxilus pilsbryi*

4³⁄₄in (12cm)

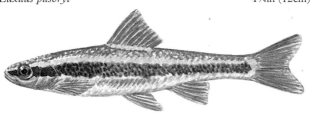

**Identification** Broad, mid-dorsal stripe. Lateral stripe running length of the body. A second dark dorso-lateral stripe above lateral stripe separated by thin iridescent gold stripe. Lacks scapular bar.
**Habitat** Upland streams with swift riffles and gravel bottoms.
**Range** Ozark Uplands of Arkansas and Missouri.


# Bleeding shiner
*Luxilus zonatus*

4³⁄₄in (12cm)

**Identification** Mid-dorsal stripe. Dark black lateral band. Iridescent gold stripe above lateral band. Crescent-shaped dark bar at cleithrum bone along rear margin of gill opening.
**Habitat** Permanent small to medium-sized upland streams in pools and riffles with moderate to swift current over gravel or rock substrates.
**Range** Northeastern Arkansas and southern Missouri.

# Rosefin shiner
*Lythrurus ardens*                                    2¾in (7cm)

**Identification** Crowded predorsal scales, more than 40 scales in lateral line, dark spot at basal portion of anterior rays of dorsal fin, and numerous dusky saddle bands over back and upper sides in males. Dark lateral band. Anal fin rays 9–11.
**Habitat** Pool areas below riffles in small to medium-sized upland streams with moderate flow and gravel or rubble substrates.
**Range** Virginia (Roanoke River) and upper and central Ohio River drainage.

# Ribbon shiner
*Lythrurus fumeus*                                    2½in (6.4cm)

**Identification** Lateral stripe intensifies posteriorly. Chin sprinkled heavily with dusky pigment. Anal rays 11–13. Lateral line strongly decurved with 35–44 scales. Predorsal scale rows 24–26.
**Habitat** Small to moderate-sized, tannin-stained streams with sand, detritus or mud bottoms in quiet backwaters.
**Range** Tennessee River basin west to Oklahoma and Texas.

# Redfin shiner
*Lythrurus umbratilis*                                    3in (7.6cm)

**Identification** Anterior dorso-lateral scales small and crowded (more than 25 predorsal rows). Lateral line decurved with 38–51 scales. Dark chevron-like markings on the anterior dorso-lateral part of the body in adults. Conspicuous black spot at origin of dorsal fin. Anal rays 9–11.
**Habitat** Small to moderately large clear, warm-water streams in sluggish pools often with aquatic vegetation over sand, gravel or rock bottoms.
**Range** Ontario; from New York and Pennsylvania, west Minnesota and south to Mississippi and Texas.


# Speckled chub
*Macrhybopsis aestivalis*                                 3in (7.6cm)

**Identification** Pale, speckled minnow. Eye small. Snout fleshy, overhangs mouth. Mouth inferior. Two or four long, conspicuous barbels. Pharyngeal teeth 4–4. Anal fin rays 7–8. Lateral line scales 34–41.
**Habitat** Swift flowing reaches of large, clear to turbid rivers and streams over sandy or gravelly substrates.
**Range** The Mississippi basin from Minnesota and Ohio south to Texas and Gulf coastal rivers from the Rio Grande to Florida.

# Sturgeon chub
*Macrhybopsis gelida*

3in (7.6cm)

**Identification** Barbeled minnow with sturgeon-like head, snout extending beyond mouth. Body pallid. Lower lobe of caudal fin darker than upper lobe, ventral margin whitish. Gular region pustulose. Pectoral fins rounded. Dorsal scales with distinct, longitudinal keels.
**Habitat** Medium-sized to large warm, turbid rivers.
**Range** Missouri River basin from Montana and Wyoming to Missouri, south to Mississippi River in Louisiana.

# Sicklefin chub
*Macrhybopsis meeki*

4in (10cm)

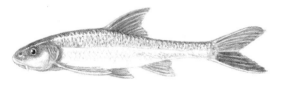

**Identification** Barbeled chub with rounded snout and pustular gular region. Body pallid. Breast scale-less. Pectoral fins long, extending well past pelvic fin insertion. Dorsal fin strongly falcate. Lower lobe of caudal fin dark with distinctive white ventral margin.
**Habitat** Large swift, warm turbid rivers over a bottom of sand or gravel.
**Range** Missouri River from North Dakota to its mouth; middle Mississippi River from latter to Louisiana.

# Silver chub
*Macrhybopsis storeriana*          8in (20cm)

**Identification** Pallid barbeled minnow. Lower lobe of caudal fin darker than upper lobe and with a distinct white ventral margin. Pharyngeal teeth 1, 4–4, 1.
**Habitat** Large, sandy-bottomed streams and rivers.
**Range** Ontario, Manitoba; through the Ohio River drainage and Mississippi basin from Wyoming south to Texas, Louisiana, and Alabama.

# Peamouth
*Mylocheilus caurinus*          14in (36cm)

**Identification** Barbeled minnow; no frenum. Dark lateral stripe from operculum to base of caudal fin. Often, second stripe from opercle to anal fin. Pelvic axillary scales well developed. Lateral line complete, with 68–79 scales. Pharyngeal teeth 1, 5–5, 1.
**Habitat** Lakes, seep channels of sluggish rivers.
**Range** British Columbia, Vancouver Island and islands off British Columbia; south to Oregon, Montana and Idaho.

# Hornyhead chub
*Nocomis biguttatus*

10in (25cm)

**Identification** Robust barbeled minnow. Breeding males with prominent red spot behind eye; head has 60–130 breeding tubercles, but no swollen crest. Anal rays 9.
**Habitat** Pools or moderate to large-sized streams and rivers with gravel substrates and moderate current.
**Range** Ontario and Manitoba, south to New York and Arkansas, west to Wyoming and Colorado.
**Comments** The hornyhead chub is a sight-feeding fish which consumes aquatic insects, crustaceans and other invertebrates and occasionally, plant material. It is a spring spawner and constructs a nest of a large pile of stones which is used for spawning and attracting other cyprinids to spawn over it.

# Bluehead chub
*Nocomis leptocephalus*

8in (20cm)

**Identification** Dark lateral band and small basicaudal spot. Breeding males with 5–15 tubercles on swollen crest between eyes. No tubercles on tip of snout. Anal fin rays 8. Pharyngeal teeth 4–4.
**Habitat** Small to medium-sized clear streams over sand, gravel, and rock substrates.
**Range** Virginia south to Georgia (Atlantic coast streams); Gulf coast drainage streams; Georgia west to Louisiana; Tennessee River system in Alabama and Mississippi.

# River chub
*Nocomis micropogon*                                    10in (25cm)

**Identification**  Barbeled chub; no red spot behind eye. Breeding
males rosy colored with 30–65 tubercles between nostrils and a snout
tip; none between eyes. Lateral line complete, 37–43 scales.
Pharyngeal teeth 4–4.
**Habitat**  Medium to large-sized streams and rivers in gravel or rock-
bottomed pools with moderate to swift current.
**Range**  Southeast Ontario; New York to Michigan, south to Alabama,
South Carolina, and Virginia.

# Golden shiner
*Notemigonus crysoleucas*                               12in (30cm)

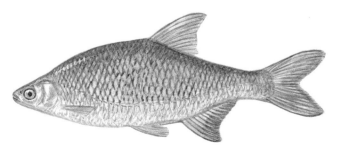

**Identification**  Deep-bodied minnow; 5–5 pharyngeal teeth. Belly
with a fleshy, naked keel extending from between the pelvic fins to the
anus. Anal fin falcate, with 11–14 rays. Lateral line decurved.
**Habitat**  Quiet waters of large impoundments, ponds, swamps and
sluggish streams over mud or sand substrates where heavy aquatic
vegetation is present.
**Range**  Native to southern Canada, and eastern North America south
to Texas. Introduced widely in the west and elsewhere.
**Comments**  The golden shiner is the most common and popular bait
fish sold in the USA. It has been readily cultured in farm ponds. In
impoundments it is an important forage fish for game fishes and
schools stay mainly near shore.

# Bigeye chub
*Notropis amblops*

3in (7.6cm)

**Identification** Barbeled minnow with large eye and conspicuous dark lateral stripe. Snout blunt, projecting beyond upper lip. Lateral line scales 33–38. Pharyngeal teeth, 1, 4–4, 1. Anal rays 8.
**Habitat** Clear rivers and streams with moderate gradients over sand, gravel or rock substrates.
**Range** Lake Ontario through Ohio Valley west to Kansas and Oklahoma and south through Tennessee to Alabama and Louisiana.

# Pallid shiner
*Notropis amnis*

2½in (6.4cm)

**Identification** Non-barbeled shiner with small, nearly horizontal mouth (upper jaw unique, nearly one-third hidden by the suborbital bone when mouth is closed). Body pallid. Anal fin rays 8. Lateral line scales 34–37.
**Habitat** Medium to large-sized silty streams and rivers; also reservoirs and oxbow lakes.
**Range** Mississippi River system from Wisconsin and Minnesota south to Louisiana and West to Guadelupe River, Texas.

# Comely shiner
*Notropis amoenus*

3½in (9cm)

**Identification** Slab-sided shiner with a faint lateral band, 10-12 anal fin rays, and large eye. Scales before dorsal fin more than 18. Lateral line with 36–42 scales. Origin of dorsal fin far behind pelvic fin insertion.
**Habitat** Channels of medium to large streams and rivers.
**Range** Atlantic coast drainage from New York to North Carolina.

## Pugnose shiner
*Notropis anogenus*                                       2in (5cm)

**Identification** Very small terminal almost vertical mouth. Dark
lateral band ending in small basicaudal spot. Pharyngeal teeth 4–4.
Anal fin rays 8. Peritoneum black.
**Habitat** Clear weedy lakes and quiet streams over clean sand or marl
substrates. Very sensitive to turbidity.
**Range** Great Lakes basin, Ontario, New York to Michigan,
Minnesota and North Dakota south to Illinois.


## Emerald shiner
*Notropis atherinoides*                                   4in (10cm)

**Identification** Strongly compressed shiner. Weakly developed lateral
stripe posteriorly. Pharyngeal teeth 2, 4–4, 2. Anal fin with 10–13 rays.
Dorsal fin situated far behind pelvic fin insertion. Lateral line scales
35–43.
**Habitat** Medium-sized to large rivers and reservoirs with clear to
turbid waters over sandy bottoms.
**Range** Northwestern and central Canada through the Plains states
and Great Lakes region to the Mississippi River system and south to
the Gulf of Mexico.


## Bridle shiner
*Notropis bifrenatus*                                     2in (5cm)

**Identification** Straw-colored shiner with a terminal oblique mouth.
Lateral band dark. Anal fin rays 7. Lateral line with 32–35 scales.
**Habitat** Clear, quiet streams with an abundance of aquatic
vegetation over silt or sand bottoms.
**Range** Atlantic drainage west through Lake Champlain to New York
and the Lake Ontario basin.

# Silverjaw minnow
*Notropis buccatus*

3½in (9cm)

**Identification** Under-surface of head distinctly flattened with numerous cavernous channels. Pale olive-yellowish. Mid-dorsal stripe prominent, anterior to dorsal fin. Anal fin rays 8.
**Habitat** Small streams and rivers in moderate current over sand or fine gravel bottoms.
**Range** Pennsylvania, Michigan, Illinois, south to Virginia, Tennessee, and Missouri; Gulf coast drainages from Georgia south to Florida and west to Louisiana.

# Ghost shiner
*Notropis buchanani*

2in (5cm)

**Identification** Uniquely pallid, slab-sided shiner. Lacks an infra-orbital canal below eye. Lateral line scales 30–35; highly elevated, especially anteriorly. Anal fin rays 8.
**Habitat** Large, warm, turbid, sluggish streams and rivers.
**Range** Mississippi River basin from Iowa to Ohio south to Alabama on the east and Mexico in the west.

# Ironcolor shiner
*Notropis chalybeaus*

2½in (6.4cm)

**Identification** Black lateral band bordered above by light-colored band. Inside mouth heavily sprinkled with black pigment. Anal fin rays 8. Pharyngeal teeth 2, 4–4, 2.
**Habitat** Acid, tannin-stained, sluggish streams and rivers.
**Range** Coastal streams from New York to Texas and north in Mississippi basin to Iowa.

# River shiner
*Notropis blennius*

4in (10cm)

**Identification** Silvery shiner with a large oblique mouth and large eye. Dorsal origin over pelvic insertion. Tip of depressed dorsal fin even with anal fin origin. Anal rays 7. Lateral line scales 34–37. Pharyngeal teeth 1 or 2, 4–4, 2 or 1.
**Habitat** Main channels of large rivers over sandy bottoms.
**Range** Alberta and Manitoba throughout northern Plains states to Ohio River basin and south throughout Mississippi River basin to Louisiana and Texas.

# Bigeye shiner
*Notropis boops*

3in (7.6cm)

**Identification** Large eye; black lateral band with clear band running just above it. Anal rays 8. Pharyngeal teeth 1, 4–4, 1. Lateral lines scales 33–39; pores outlined in black. Scales on dorso-lateral region dark-edged.
**Habitat** Moderate-sized to large streams with fairly high gradients over gravel, rocks, or clean sand substrates.
**Range** The lower Ohio River basin to Tennessee in the south and through the central Mississippi drainage to Kansas and Oklahoma.

# Dusky shiner
*Notropis cummingsae*

2½in (6.4cm)

**Identification** Dark lateral band and small basicaudal spot. Body olive dorsally and silvery with light band of coppery brown. Tip of chin dark. Anal rays 9–11.
**Habitat** Lowland tannin-stained streams.
**Range** North Carolina south to eastern Florida; disjunct in western Florida and middle Chattahoochee drainage, Alabama and Georgia.

# Bigmouth shiner
*Notropis dorsalis*

2½in (6.4cm)

**Identification** Lateral band distinct, particularly on caudal peduncle. Distinct dark mid-dorsal stripe. Pair of crescents between nostrils. Anal rays 8.
**Habitat** Shallow, open, prairie-like streams with sand bottoms.
**Range** Southern Manitoba, eastern Wyoming, and Colorado east to New York, West Virginia, south to Missouri and Illinois.

# Blacknose shiner
*Notropis heterodon*

2½in (6.4cm)

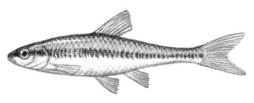

**Identification** Dark lateral band forming a zig-zag pattern extending onto head, through the eye and around snout onto chin. Chin black.
**Habitat** Clear, clean weedy waters.
**Range** Great Lakes basin, barely penetrating southern Canada and extending south to Illinois and Kentucky and east to New York.

# Bluehead shiner
*Notropis hubbsi*

2½in (6.4cm)

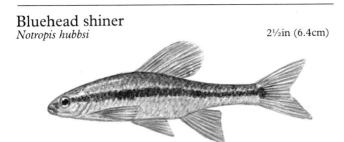

**Identification** A beautiful, distinctive, slab-sided shiner with 9–10 dorsal fin rays, large eye, terminal mouth, broad black lateral band terminating in a large basicaudal spot. Chin distinctly black pigmented. Anal rays 9–11. Pharyngeal teeth 4–4. Lateral line incomplete with 2–9 pored scales. Lateral series of 34–36 scales.
**Habitat** Quiet backwater areas of small to medium-sized sluggish streams and oxbow lakes.
**Range** Mississippi River valley from central Louisiana north to Arkansas and southwestern Illinois.

# Spottail shiner
*Notropis hudsonius*

6in (15cm)

**Identification** A stout-bodied, laterally compressed shiner with a bluntly triangular head, blunt snout, large eye, moderately large mouth and basicaudal spot. Dorsum yellowish or golden with silvery sides and faint lateral stripe terminating in a spot. Caudal fin with whitish lower rays. Anal rays 8. Lateral line complete with 38–42 scales.
**Habitat** Small streams, rivers and lakes over gravel, rock and sand substrates.
**Range** Canada from Northwest Territories to southern Canada, Atlantic coast from Massachusetts to Georgia, west to the Dakotas, Mississippi River basin south to Missouri.

# Taillight shiner
*Notropis maculatus*

2¾in (7cm)

**Identification** Dark lateral band extends from snout to large basicaudal spot. Dorso-lateral scales dark-edged. Anal rays 8. Pharyngeal teeth 4–4.
**Habitat** Shallow, tannin–stained waters of low-gradient streams, sloughs, lakes, including oxbows and swamps in vegetated areas over mud or silt bottoms.
**Range** From Missouri and Oklahoma to the Gulf coast, east to Florida and north along Atlantic coast to North Carolina.


# Ozark minnow
*Notropis nubilus*

3in (7.6cm)

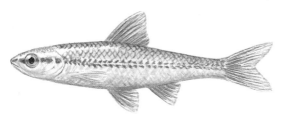

**Identification** A slender, terete minnow with moderately large eye, small head, blunt snout and subterminal, slightly oblique mouth. Dark lateral band. Basicaudal spot present. Dorso-lateral scales outlined with dark pigment. Anal fins 8. Pharyngeal teeth 4–4. Intestine long, coiled. Black peritoneum.
**Habitat** Clear, spring-fed, small to medium-sized streams with high gradients over gravel or rock substrates.
**Range** Minnesota and Wisconsin south to Oklahoma and Arkansas.

# Ozark shiner
*Notropis ozarcanus*                                     2¾in (7cm)

**Identification** Dorsal scales conspicuously dark-edged. Anal rays 8.
Pharyngeal teeth 4–4. Lateral line scales 34–38, the anterior ones
much deeper than adjacent scales. Rear margin of anterior lateral line
scales slightly scalloped.
**Habitat** Swift sections below riffles in moderate current in large
streams and rivers.
**Range** Ozark Uplands of Missouri, Arkansas and Oklahoma.

# Silver shiner
*Notropis photogenis*                                    5in (13cm)

**Identification** Dark silvery band; anal rays 10–13, 34–40 lateral line
scales, and 2, 4–4, 2 pharyngeal teeth. Origin of dorsal fin directly
over pelvic fin insertion. Crescent-shaped markings between nostrils.
**Habitat** Large, clear streams with moderate current.
**Range** Lake Erie drainage, Ontario, and western New York south to
Tennessee and Georgia.

# Rosyface shiner
*Notropis rubellus*

3½in (9cm)

**Identification** A slender, somewhat compressed, silvery minnow with moderately long head. Iridescent-green stripe above the lateral line. Lateral band dusky. Anterior lateral line pores black-edged. Anal fin rays 10–13. Predorsal scales 17–21.

**Habitat** Clear pools and riffles of large creeks to small rivers with moderate current over gravel or rock.

**Range** Quebec west through Great Lakes drainage to Manitoba; south to Oklahoma, Arkansas and southern Alabama.

# Sabine shiner
*Notropis sabinae*

2½in (6.4cm)

**Identification** Straw-colored shiner with ventral, almost horizontal mouth, small eye, bluntly rounded snout, pharyngeal teeth 4–4, and seven anal rays. Lateral line scales 31–37. Eyes directed upward. Dorso-lateral scales outlined with pigment.

**Habitat** Small streams and rivers in slight to moderate current over fine, silt-free sand substrates.

**Range** Southeast Texas and Louisiana; disjunctly in northeastern Arkansas and southeastern Missouri.

# Silverband shiner
*Notropis shumardi*

2½in (6.4cm)

**Identification** A pale, moderately deep-bodied compressed fish with a small head, large eye, and short, rounded snout. Body coloration pale olive-yellow with silvery sides and white belly. Silvery lateral band. Predorsal stripe thin. Anal fin rays 8–9. Pharyngeal teeth 2, 4–4, 2. Lateral line scales 34–37.
**Habitat** Main channels of large rivers in swift current over sand or gravel bars.
**Range** Mississippi River basin from south Dakota and Illinois to Louisiana, and Gulf coast rivers to Alabama and Texas.

# Sand shiner
*Notropis stramineus*

3in (7.6cm)

**Identification** A moderately deep-bodied, robust, pale-colored shiner with short head, large eyes directed laterally. Pallid to straw-colored. Faint lateral band on caudal peduncle. Tiny basicaudal spot present. Anal rays 7. Pharyngeal teeth 4–4. Lateral line scales 33–37.
**Habitat** Clear to turbid, sand-bottomed streams and rivers.
**Range** From St Lawrence drainage to Montana in the north and through the Mississippi basin south to Texas and in Gulf coast streams to Mexico.

# Telescope shiner
*Notropis telescopus*                                    3in (7.6cm)

**Identification** Back with intense broad black mid-dorsal stripe and conspicuous dark edging on scales. Dorso-lateral areas with faint, wavy dark lines converging behind dorsal fin. Pores of lateral line outlined with dark pigment. Anal rays 9–11.
**Habitat** Clear upland streams in pools near riffles with gravel or rocky bottoms.
**Range** Upland regions east and west of Mississippi River; east in Tennessee River system in Tennessee, North Carolina, Virginia, and Kentucky; west in Arkansas and Missouri uplands.


# Weed shiner
*Notropis texanus*                                       3in (7.6cm)

**Identification** Dark lateral stripe from snout tip to caudal base. Anal rays 7. Pharyngeal teeth 2, 4–4, 2. Light colored zone just above dark lateral band. Small, basicaudal spot present.
**Habitat** Clear, lowland streams of small to moderate size with sand and mud bottoms, some current and aquatic vegetation.
**Range** Minnesota, Wisconsin, and Michigan south to Florida and west to Texas in Gulf Coastal drainages.

# Mimic shiner
*Notropis volucellus*

2¼in (5.8cm)

**Identification** Dorsal scales outlined. Anal rays 8. Pharyngeal teeth 4–4. Anterior scales in lateral line higher than long and higher than scales in adjacent rows. Infraorbital canal beneath eye complete.
**Habitat** Lakes and medium to large streams and rivers in current over sand, gravel or hard bottom.
**Range** From southern Canada through the St Lawrence and Great Lakes Region south to North Carolina and throughout the Mississippi River basin to Texas and Mississippi. Gulf Coast rivers to Mexico.


# Pugnose minnow
*Opsopoeodus emiliae*

2½in (6.4cm)

**Identification** Very small, nearly vertical mouth; nine dorsal rays. Dorsal and lateral scales distinctly outlined with dark melanophores. Narrow dark lateral band. Pharyngeal teeth 5–5.
**Habitat** Clear, vegetated, quiet regions of sluggish streams, sloughs, or oxbow over mud, sand or debris substrates.
**Range** From lower Great Lakes drainage through the Mississippi River system to Gulf of Mexico from Mexico to Texas.

# Suckermouth minnow
*Phenacobius mirabilis*  4in (10cm)

**Identification** Blunt snout; inferior sucker-like mouth, and dusky lateral band extending from the head to end of the caudal peduncle, terminating in a conspicuous black blotch. Anal rays 7. Pharyngeal teeth 4–4.
**Habitat** Riffle inhabitant of sand and gravel-bottomed, permanent medium to large streams of moderate gradient.
**Range** Central Mississippi Valley from Wisconsin to Pennsylvania south to Oklahoma and Texas and northern Alabama.


# Stargazing minnow
*Phenacobius uranops*  4½in (11cm)

**Identification** Long, rounded snout; ventral, sucker-like mouth. Small barbels above the upper lip. Narrow dark lateral band terminating in distinct basicaudal spot. Anal rays 7. Breast and belly scaleless.
**Habitat** Swift riffles of gravel and rock-bottomed streams and rivers.
**Range** Green, Cumberland, and upper Tennessee River drainages of Virginia, Kentucky, Georgia, and Alabama.

# Northern redbelly dace
*Phoxinus eos*                                        3in (7.6cm)

**Identification** Two lateral bands uniting on caudal peduncle. Origin
of dorsal fin distinctly posterior to pelvic fin insertion. Pharyngeal
teeth 5–5. Lateral line incomplete, 70–90 in lateral series. Peritoneum
black.
**Habitat** Boggy creeks, ponds, and lakes.
**Range** British Columbia to Hudson Bay drainage and Nova Scotia,
south to Colorado, Montana, Minnesota, and Pennsylvania. Isolated
populations in Nebraska.


# Southern redbelly dace
*Phoxinus erythrogaster*                              2½in (6.4cm)

**Identification** Two conspicuous dusky lateral stripes, a broad one
just below the midline of the side and a narrower one situated above
(light-colored area between). Lateral line with 70–95 in lateral series.
**Habitat** Clear, cool, gravel-bottomed, spring-fed brooks, springs, and
small headwater streams with moderate to swift current.
**Range** Central Mississippi Valley from Wisconsin to Pennsylvania
south to Oklahoma and northern Alabama.

# Finescale dace
*Phoxinus neogeaus*                                    3in (7.6cm)

**Identification** Dark lateral band. Breeding males flushed with single
red on venter. Peritoneum back. Pharyngeal teeth in two rows.
**Habitat** Bog ponds, streams and lakes.
**Range** New Brunswick, Maine, and New Hampshire through
southern Quebec and New York to Michigan northwest in the
Mackenzie River system to the Arctic Circle. Isolated populations in
Wyoming, Colorado, and Nebraska.


# Mountain redbelly dace
*Phoxinus oreas*                                      2½in (6.4cm)

**Identification** Distinctive black lateral band from opercle to anal fin
base. Bordered above by creamy stripe and followed by a narrow black
stripe on the rear half of the body. Upper sides with large, black spots.
Anal rays 8.
**Habitat** Small, swift mountain streams over sand, gravel, or rock
substrates.
**Range** Atlantic Coast drainages from Virginia to North Carolina, also
Upper Tennessee River drainage in east Tennessee.

# Bluntnose minnow
*Pimephales notatus*                    3in (7.6cm)

**Identification** Distinctive black lateral band. Dorso-lateral scales outlined with black. Basicaudal spot distinct. First dorsal fin ray short, splint-like. Predorsal area flattened with scales small and crowded. Peritoneum black. Lateral line complete.
**Habitat** Medium to large-sized clear streams and lakes over sand, gravel, or rock substrates with aquatic vegetation.
**Range** Quebec west to Manitoba; New York south to Georgia; through Great Lakes and Mississippi Valley drainages.

# Fathead minnow
*Pimephales promelas*                    3in (7.6cm)

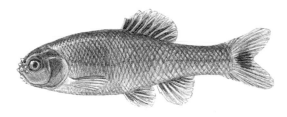

**Identification** Body robust. Basicaudal spot absent or indistinct. Scales small and crowded in predorsal region. First dorsal fin ray short, splint-like. Peritoneum black. Lateral line incomplete.
**Habitat** Small streams, ditches, ponds, and lakes over soft mud or sand bottom.
**Range** Throughout central North America, west to the Appalachians south into Mexico. Introduced widely.

# Bullhead minnow
*Pimephales vigilax*                                    3in (7.6cm)

**Identification** Scales crowded before dorsal fin, spot on anterior membranes of dorsal fin. Large, wedge-shaped basicaudal spot. Distinctive crescent-shaped dark mark on each side above upper lip on snout. Upper lip only slightly thickened at middle. Lateral lime complete. Peritoneum silvery.
**Habitat** Large, sluggish, turbid streams and rivers over sand and mud substrates.
**Range** Mississippi basin from Minnesota and Pennsylvania in the north, southward west of the Appalachians to Georgia and Texas.

# Woundfin
*Plagopterus argentissimus*                             3in (7.6cm)

**Identification** Barbeled cyprinid with an overhanging snout, two spines, seven rays in dorsal fin, and deeply embedded scales. Back with small black dots. Origin of dorsal fin posterior to pelvic fin insertion. Pharyngeal teeth 1, 5–4, 1.
**Habitat** Swift, turbid, sand-bottomed streams.
**Range** Virgin River in Utah, Arizona and Nevada; Moapa River, Nevada.

# Flathead chub
*Platygobio gracilis*

9in (23cm)

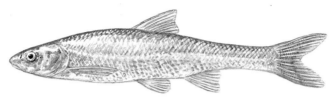

**Identification** Barbeled chub. Dorsal and pectoral fins falcate. Breast scaled. Pharyngeal teeth 2, 4-4, 2. Lower lobe of caudal fin dusky. Lateral line scales 42-56.
**Habitat** Large, turbid rivers over firm sand, or gravel substrate in moderate to swift current.
**Range** Mackenzie River in Canada south through the Plains states to Louisiana and west to New Mexico.

# Sacramento squawfish
*Ptychocheilus grandis*

36in (91cm)

**Identification** Large non-barbeled cyprinid, with a tapered (pike-like) head. Sides silvery-gray. Dorsal rays 8, anal rays 8. Lateral line complete with 73–81 scales. Pharyngeal teeth 2, 5–4, 2.
**Habitat** Streams, rivers and lakes over rock and sand substrates in deep pools.
**Range** North and central California.

# Colorado squawfish
*Ptychocheilus lucius*                                      5ft (1.5m)

**Identification** Flattened head, small eye and large, terminal mouth.
Young have wedge-shaped caudal spot. Dorsal fin rays 9. Lateral line
decurved, complete with 80–95 scales.
**Habitat** Deep, swift sections of turbid large streams and in large pools
over sand, gravel or rock substrates.
**Range** Colorado River basin, in Wyoming, Colorado, and Utah south
to Arizona, California, and Mexico.
**Comments** The Colorado squawfish at 5ft (1.5m) in length holds the
distinction of being the largest minnow in North America.
Unfortunately, habitat alteration and the introduction of exotic fishes
in the Colorado River basin have resulted in its precipitous decline.
Today, it has been placed on the US Endangered Species List.

# Northern squawfish
*Ptychocheilus oregonensis*                                12in (30cm)

**Identification** Long head, small eye, and long snout. Dorsal fin
origin slightly behind pelvic insertion. Dorsal fin rays 9–10. Anal rays
8. Lateral line scales 65–77.
**Habitat** Lakes, preferring still waters.
**Range** Pacific Slope from Oregon north to British Columbia.

# Blacknose dace
*Rhinichthys atratulus*

3½in (9cm)

**Identification** Barbeled; snout long. Body yellowish olive to dark brown with blotches on sides; dark lateral band. Anal fin rays 7.
**Habitat** Springs and cool, clear, gravel-bottomed streams with swift current.
**Range** Canada, Nova Scotia west to Manitoba; New England south to South Carolina, Georgia, and Alabama, west to North Dakota and Nebraska.

# Longnose dace
*Rhinichthys cataractae*

7in (18cm)

**Identification** Barbeled minnow. Long bulbous snout projecting far beyond mouth; small eye; small, ventral mouth. Wide black lateral band. Anal rays 7. Caudal peduncle deep, long.
**Habitat** Swift, gravel-bottomed riffles of streams and lakes.
**Range** Canada, Northern USA south in Appalachians to Georgia, south in Rockies to the Rio Grande, Texas and New Mexico.

# Speckled dace
*Rhinichthys osulus*

4in (10cm)

**Identification** Barbeled; small, ventral mouth; small eyes; and moderately pointed snout. Grayish-green sides with dark blotches or speckles. Bases of fins reddish in breeding males. Anal rays 7. Lateral line with 60–90 scales.
**Habitat** Desert springs; small streams, rivers and lakes.
**Range** British Columbia south to Arizona.

# Redside shiner
*Richardsonius balteatus*

7in (18cm)

**Identification** Deep-bodied, compressed; no barbels. Upper sides with depigmented stripe bordered below by dark/lateral stripe. Dorsal rays 9. Origin of dorsal fin posterior to pelvic fin insertion. Anal fin with 10–22 rays. Lateral line complete with 55–67 scales.
**Habitat** Sluggish streams and rivers; also ponds and lakes in areas of abundant aquatic vegetation.
**Range** British Columbia and Alberta south to Oregon, Nevada and Utah. Introduced in Colorado River drainage.

# Creek chub
*Semotilus atromaculatus*                                    12in (30cm)

**Identification** Very large mouth; black spot at anterior base of dorsal
fin; dark lateral band ending in small basicaudal spot. Small, flat-like
barbel in the groove above the upper lip. Anterior body scales
crowded.
**Habitat** Small, clear headwater streams and lakes over sand, gravel,
or rock substrates.
**Range** Occurs throughout most of USA east of the Rockies.


# Fallfish
*Semotilus corporalis*                                        4in (10cm)

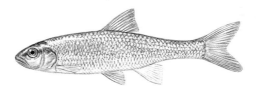

**Identification** Barbeled; mouth overhung by snout. Sides have series
of dark, crescent-shaped or triangular black bars at the base of each
scale along the sides. Scales large, not crowded anteriad.
**Habitat** Clear, flowing, gravel-bottomed streams and lakes.
**Range** New Brunswick, Quebec, and Ontario, east to the
Appalachians to Virginia.

# Suckers – Catostomidae

Suckers are soft-rayed, bottom-dwelling fishes with a sucker-like, protractile mouth with fleshy protrusible lips, high dorsal ray count (ten or more rays) and an anal fin positioned far back on the caudal peduncle. There are 59 North American species.

## Carpsucker
*Carpiodes carpio*

20in (51cm)

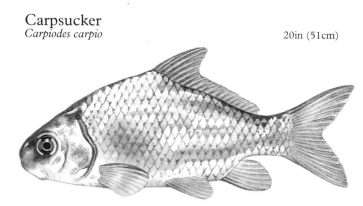

**Identification** Deep-bodied; small inferior mouth, high-arched back. Lower lip with small knob presents at its middle. Dorsal fin long (22–30 rays) and falcate. Pelvic and anal fins without black pigment. Subopercle bone subtriangular. Maximum size about 10lbs (4.5kg).
**Habitat** Moderate to large streams, rivers, and reservoirs in quiet backwater pools.
**Range** Great Plains from Montana to Texas through Mississippi basin northeast to Ohio.

# Quillback
*Carpiodes cyprinus*

19in (48cm)

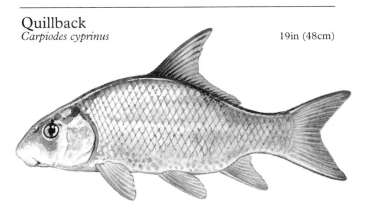

**Identification** Arched back, subtriangular subopercle, long falcate dorsal fin (its depressed length almost as long or longer than dorsal fin base). Mouth far forward on head, upper jaw not extending past front of eye. Mouth without nipple-like knob on lower lip. Maximum size about 3lb 8oz (1.6kg).
**Habitat** Clear, large streams with pools and stable gravel bottoms.
**Range** Atlantic Coast drainages from St Lawrence River south to Georgia; Gulf Coastal drainages to Louisiana; north in Mississippi River basin to North Dakota and southern Canada, east through Great Lakes to New York.

# Highfin carpsucker
*Carpiodes velifer*

12in (30cm)

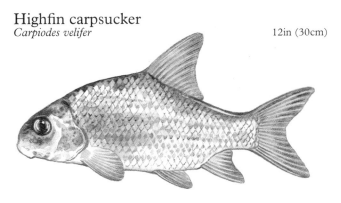

**Identification** Compressed; arched back, preopercle subtriangular, distinctly long dorsal fin (23–27 rays), the first ray when depressed reaching beyond the back of the fin base. Mouth ventral and lower lip with nipple-like knob.
**Habitat** Clear streams and rivers with firm substrates; also reservoirs.
**Range** Mississippi River system from Nebraska and Ohio in the north to Oklahoma and western Florida in the south.

# Longnose sucker
*Catostomus catostomus*

25in (64cm)

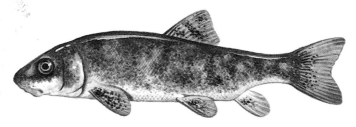

**Identification** Elongate; small eye; snout terminating in a rounded point; ventral protrusible mouth, lips with coarse round papillae. Dorsal fin rays 9–11; lateral line scales small, 99–108.
**Habitat** Clear, cold lakes and rivers.
**Range** From Alaska east throughout Canada south to Maryland, Pennsylvania and Minnesota west to northern Colorado and Washington.

# White sucker
*Catostomus commersoni*

18in (46cm)

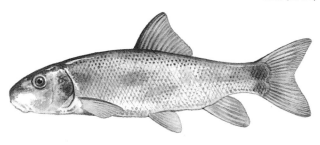

**Identification** Slender; fleshy papillose lips, short dorsal fin (11–13 rays), rounded snout, and area between eyes flat, not concave. Lateral line scales small, 55–76 in lateral line. Size about 6–7lbs (2.7–3.2kg).
**Range** North America east of Rockies from Hudson Bay in the north to Oklahoma, northern Mississippi and northern Georgia in the south.

# Mountain sucker
*Catostomus platyrhynchus*                                    8in (20cm)

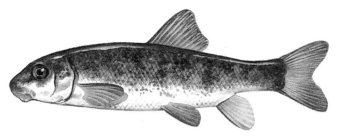

**Identification** Ventral, protrusible mouth with large papillose lips.
Cartilaginous sheath of lower jaw obvious even when mouth closed.
Black lateral band and/or fine dorsal blotches of black pigment. Dorsal
fin rays 9–11. Lateral line scales 60–108.
**Habitat** Clear streams in shallow water of moderate current over
rubble bottoms. Rarely in lakes.
**Range** Mountainous region of western North America from western
Saskatchewan and British Columbia south to Nevada and Utah and
California.

# Blue sucker
*Cycleptus elongatus*                                         40in (1m)

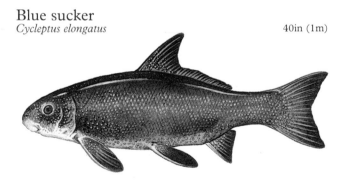

**Identification** Streamlined; falcate dorsal fin with 28–35 rays, inferior
mouth with papillose lips. Body blue black. Lateral line scales 53–58.
Maximum size about 6lbs (2.7kg).
**Habitat** Deep, fast-flowing rivers and channels of lakes over a firm
bottom.
**Range** Mississippi River system, from Minnesota and Ohio south to
Texas and in Louisiana, Alabama west to New Mexico.

# Creek chubsucker
*Erimyzon oblongus*

9in (22.8cm)

**Identification** Robust; no lateral line (39–41 lateral scale rows);
oblique mouth less inferior than most suckers. Lower lip plicate.
Dorsal fin rounded with 10 rays. Anal fin of males double-lobed with
7 rays.
**Habitat** Small creeks and streams of moderate gradient with soft
bottoms and aquatic vegetation.
**Range** Eastern USA from New Brunswick to Florida and west to
Texas and Iowa.

# Lake chubsucker
*Erimyzon sucetta*

11½in (29cm)

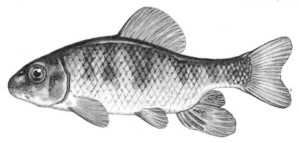

**Identification** Robust; lacks lateral line; short round dorsal fin
(11–12 rays); nearly terminal mouth with plicate lips. Eye small.
Young with dark black lateral band. Lateral line scale rows 35–37.
**Habitat** Quiet, heavily vegetated areas of oxbow lakes, sloughs of
large rivers, and sluggish stream backwaters.
**Range** Atlantic Coast drainages from Virginia to Florida, Gulf
Coastal drainage from Florida to Texas and Mississippi River Valley
from Louisiana north to Wisconsin; Great Lakes region.

# Northern hog sucker
*Hypentelium nigricans*

12in (30cm)

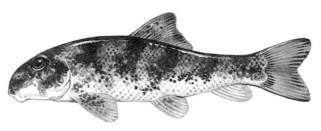

**Identification** Mottled; large-headed sucker with papillose lips.
Ventral mouth. Concave between the eyes. Four to six dark saddles
cross back extending obliquely forward onto the sides. Dorsal fin rays
11. Lateral line scales 46–50.
**Habitat** Riffles and pools below riffles in clear, permanent streams
with gravel or rocky bottoms.
**Range** Ontario; Eastern USA excluding southern Georgia, Florida,
and Alabama.

# Smallmouth buffalo
*Ictiobus bubalus*

36in (91cm)

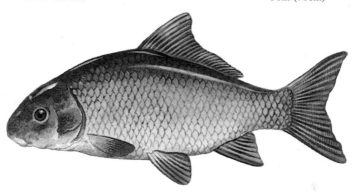

**Identification** Compressed; high-arched back, small mouth, long
dorsal fin (25–31 rays. Pelvic fins grayish black, other fins dusky.
Anterior rays of dorsal fin long, less than half length of fin base.
Subopercle semicircular. Lips plicate. Maximum size to 51lbs
(23.1kg).
**Habitat** Large streams and rivers with moderate current; lakes and
reservoirs.
**Range** Mississippi River basin from Gulf Coast states north to Ohio
and the Dakotas, west to Rio Grande.

# Largemouth buffalo
*Ictiobus cyprinellus*                                    35in (89cm)

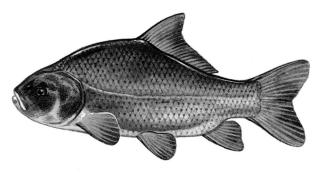

**Identification** Deep-bodied; terminal oblique mouth, thin lips; long sickle-shaped dorsal fin (23–32 rays). Front of upper lip level with lower margin of eye. Subopercle semicircular. All fins blackish. Back weakly keeled or rounded. Maximum size 80lbs (36.3kg).
**Habitat** Deep pools of large streams and rivers, oxbow lakes, and reservoirs.
**Range** Mississippi River Valley from Minnesota and Ohio in the north to Alabama and Texas in the south.


# Black buffalo
*Ictiobus niger*                                          25in (64cm)

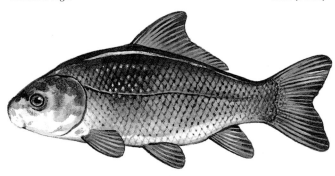

**Identification** Robust; less arched dorsal contour, small subterminal mouth (anterior tip of mouth far below the lower margin of eye). Upper lip thick, deeply grooved. Dorsal fin long (27–31 rays) not sickle-shaped. All fins dark. Maximum size 36lbs (15.9kg)
**Habitat** Strong currents of large rivers and impoundments.
**Range** Mississippi River Valley from Nebraska to Ohio, south to Alabama and Texas.

# Spotted sucker
*Minytrema melanops*                                    18in (46cm)

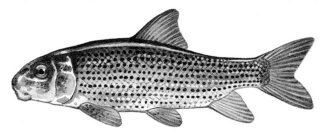

**Identification** Slim-bodied; incomplete or absent lateral line (42–46 scales in lateral series) conspicuous black spot at the base of each scale on body forming parallel rows. Lips plicate. Mouth inferior.
**Habitat** Clear to slightly turbid streams with submerged aquatic vegetation and soft substrates. Also found in sloughs, lakes and reservoirs.
**Range** Throughout most of eastern USA west to eastern portions of the Great Plains states and north to Minnesota.

# Silver redhorse
*Moxostoma anisurum*                                    22in (56cm)

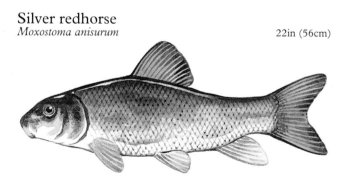

**Identification** Convex or straight-edged dorsal fin (14–16 rays), ventral mouth with lower lip distinctly bi-lobed and papillose, its posterior margin forming an acute V-shaped angle. Caudal fins slate colored.
**Habitat** Large and deep sluggish pools of moderate-sized, clear streams and large rivers over rocky or gravelly substrates.
**Range** Atlantic Slope from Virginia to Georgia, throughout Ohio basin, Ozark Uplands, upper Mississippi and Great Lakes-St Lawrence regions to Hudson Bay drainage.

# River redhorse
*Moxostoma carinatum*                                  30in (76cm)

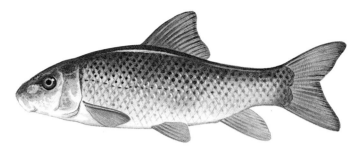

**Identification** Ventral mouth; small eye. Caudal fin bright red; base
with a thin black pencil line along the margin of the last scale row.
Lips plicate, rear margin of lower lip almost straight. Weighs up to
16lbs (16.kg).
**Habitat** Pools and swift main channel regions of clear, medium to
large-sized streams and rivers over gravel or rock substrates.
**Range** Great Lakes drainages and St Lawrence River in Quebec,
Ontario, Michigan and Ohio; central Mississippi River basin; Mobile
basin.


# Black redhorse
*Moxostoma duquesnei*                                  15in (38cm)

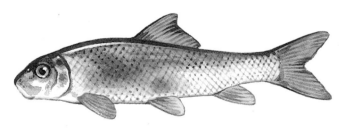

**Identification** Slender; concave dorsal fin (12–14), mouth with thin
plicate lips; slender caudal peduncle. Rear margin of lower lip almost
straight or forming a broad obtuse angle. Pelvic rays usually 10.
**Habitat** Clear, medium-sized streams with gravel and rock bottoms.
 **Range** Mississippi and Great Lakes drainages from St Lawrence
River west to Iowa, south to Oklahoma and across Gulf States to
western Florida.

## Golden redhorse
*Moxostoma erythrurum*

24in (61cm)

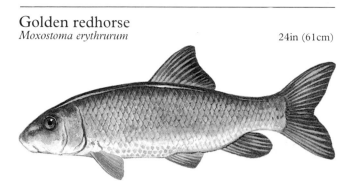

**Identification** Plicate lower lips; usually nine pelvic rays. Rear margin of lower lip forming a distinctly acute V-shaped angle. Caudal fin slate colored.
**Habitat** Clear, gravel-bottomed streams and rivers.
**Range** Ontario; Atlantic Coast drainages from Maryland to North Carolina; New York west to Minnesota and North Dakota, south to Texas and Mississippi; Mobile Bay drainage.


## Shorthead redhorse
*Moxostoma macrolepidotum*

24in (61cm)

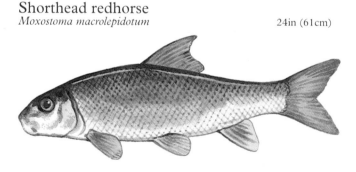

**Identification** Small mouth with deeply plicate lips (posterior margin of lower lip nearly straight). Unique "pea"-shaped thickening at middle of upper lip. Pelvic rays 9. Scales of dorsum and upper sides with a crescent-shaped dark spot at base. Caudal fin bright red.
**Habitat** Moderately large rivers having gravelly or rocky bottoms and permanent strong flow.
**Range** Central Canada east to St Lawrence region, south through Great Lakes to Mississippi basin (Oklahoma and Arkansas).

# Blacktail redhorse
*Moxostoma poecilurum*                    18in (46cm)

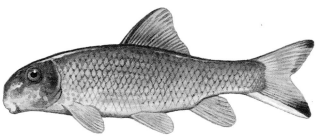

**Identification** Slender; distinctive caudal fin, lobe with blackened horizontal stripe bordered by white on lower edge. Lips plicate. Breast fully scaled.
**Habitat** Tannin-stained, lowland streams and rivers with sand and gravel substrates.
**Range** Gulf Coast drainages from Florida west to eastern Texas; Mississippi River system in Arkansas and Tennessee.

# Striped jumprock
*Moxostoma rupiscartes*                    10in (25cm)

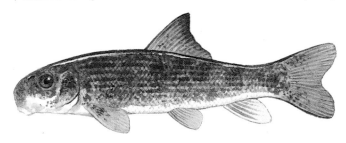

**Identification** Elongate; ventral mouth, plicate lips. Large flattened head. Striped pattern faint on sides. Young with dark blotches. Pelvic fin rays 9. Caudal fin yellowish with rounded lobes. Lateral line complete with 45–50 scales.
**Habitat** Moderate to swift riffle areas of small sand or gravel-bottomed streams.
**Range** North Carolina to Georgia.

# Greater redhorse
*Moxostoma valenciennesi*                          18in (46cm)

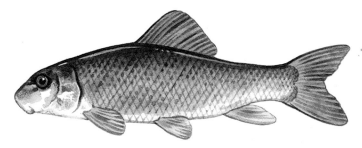

**Identification** Large, compressed sucker with greatest depth of body at dorsal fin origin. Inferior protrusible mouth not overhung by snout; plicate lips. Dorsal, caudal, and anal fins dark red. Dorsal fin rays 13. Lateral line scales 42–45.
**Habitat** Large clear streams with clean sand, gravel or boulder substrates.
**Range** Central and eastern North America in the upper Mississippi River and Great Lake-St Lawrence system.

# Razorback sucker
*Xyrauchen texanus*                                36in (91cm)

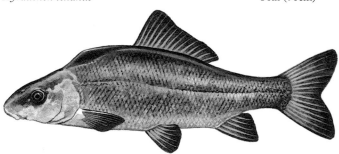

**Identification** Bluish-black sucker with long head, fleshy snout, ventral mouth, and predorsal area with high sharp ridges from head to dorsal fin. Dorsal fin rays 12–15, origin anterior to pelvic fin insertion. Lateral line with 68  87 scales.
**Habitat** Large rivers and reservoirs over mud, sand, or gravel substrates.
**Range** Colorado River system of Wyoming, Arizona and California.

# Catfishes – Ictaluridae

North American catfishes (39 species) are characterized by four pairs of barbels, scaleless body, a wide mouth with hundreds of minute teeth arranged in bands on the roof of the mouth and adipose fin. All species possess venomous spines at the origins of the dorsal and pectoral fins which can inflict a nasty wound.

## Black bullhead
*Ameiurus melas*                                                17in (43cm)

**Identification** Adipose fin free; caudal fin almost square or with a slightly notch. Brownish yellow to black above, yellowish-white belly. No mottling. Chin barbels grayish to black. Anal fin rays 17–21. Generally less than 1lb (0.5kg).
**Habitat** Oxbows, lakes and reservoirs and backwater areas of streams over a mud bottom.
**Range** Ontario west to Saskatchewan; most of the central USA east of the Rockies, except for eastern coastal states.

# Yellow bullhead
*Ameiurus natalis*

18in (46cm)

**Identification** Robust; whitish chin barbels, deep caudal peduncle, and a free adipose fin. No mottling. Anal fin 24–27 rays. Usually less than 1lb (0.5kg) in weight.
**Habitat** Clear, gravel or rocky-bottomed, permanent streams in areas with heavy vegetation. Also found in ponds and lakes.
**Range** Ontario, eastern USA, east to the eastern Great Plains.

# Brown bullhead
*Ictalurus nebulosus*

19in (48cm)

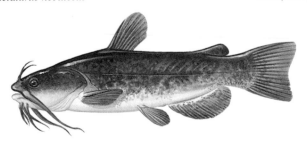

**Identification** Free adipose fin; emarginate caudal fin. Body olivaceous with strong mottling. Chin barbels darkly pigmented. Anal fin rays 21–24.
**Habitat** Farm ponds, lakes, and reservoirs; also streams and rivers in deep pools with submerged logs and overhanging banks.
**Range** Nova Scotia west to Saskatchewan; eastern USA from North Dakota to Arkansas in the west and north to Maine in the east. Widely introduced.

# Blue catfish
*Ictalurus furcatus*

44in (1.1m)

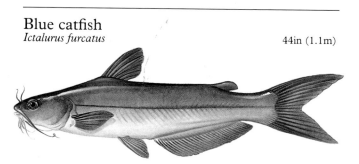

**Identification** Sloping, wedge-shaped head, prominent hump anterior to dorsal fin, deeply forked tail, and adipose fin. Body bluish-gray. Four pairs of barbels. Anal fin straight-edged with 30–35 rays. Maximum size of over 100lbs (45.4kg).
**Habitat** Large rivers and large lakes in deeper, swifter portions over rock, gravel, or clean sand substrates.
**Range** Mississippi River system; Georgia west to Mexico; widely introduced.

# Channel catfish
*Ictalurus punctatus*

47in (1.2m)

**Identification** Deeply forked tail; free adipose fin. Body gray blue; small dark spots randomly scattered on sides. Anal fin rounded with 24–29 rays.
**Habitat** Large streams and rivers in slow to moderate current over sand, gravel, or rock substrates. Also ponds, lakes, reservoirs.
**Range** Quebec west to Alberta; entire east-central USA from Rockies to just west of Appalachians. Widely introduced throughout USA.
**Comments** This favorite of anglers is one of the foremost sport fishes. Recently commercial catfish farming has been initiated in southern areas such as Arkansas and Mississippi resulting in tens of millions of dollars being added to state economies. Food of the channel catfish includes fish, insects, mollusks, and crayfish.

# Ozark madtom
*Noturus albater*                                    5in (13cm)

**Identification** Slender madtom; nine soft pectoral rays; adipose fin forming a low keel-like ridge and possessing a large dark bar. Pectoral spine short with well-developed posterior serrae. Fins and body mottled with four indistinct dark bars crossing dorsum.
**Habitat** Clear, swift, moderate to large-sized streams with gravel, rock or rubble substrates in riffles and pools.
**Range** Ozark Uplands of Missouri and Arkansas (White, Little Red, and St Francis drainages).

# Mountain madtom
*Noturus eleutherus*                                 4in (10cm)

**Identification** Conspicuously mottled body, flattened head, and adipose fin high and almost free posteriorly from caudal fin. No discrete black blotch in dorsal fin. Pectoral rays 8; pectoral spine long with 5–8 posterior serrae recurved toward base; anterior serrae well developed.
**Habitat** Large, clear, swift to moderately flowing streams and rivers.
**Range** Ohio and Tennessee River systems; Ouachita River system of Arkansas and Little River system of Oklahoma and Arkansas.

# Slender madtom
*Noturus exilis*

6in (15cm)

**Identification** Slender, brownish. Nearly equal jaws, nine pelvic rays, and five to eight long, straight serrae along posterior edge of pectoral spine. Anal rays 17–22. Adipose fin long, low keel–like.
**Habitat** Small to moderate-sized streams and small rivers with moderate to swift current, clear water, and rock or gravel-bottomed riffles.
**Range** Central Mississippi River system (Ozark and Tennessee highlands) extending to Iowa and Minnesota in the north.

# Stonecat
*Noturus flavus*

12in (30cm)

**Identification** Unicolored; premaxillary tooth patch on upper jaw with backward extension. Caudal fin with upper and lower rays lighter than rest of fin.
**Habitat** Gravel-bottomed or rocky substrates in moderate to large streams; also known from lakes.
**Range** St Lawrence River drainage west to Alberta; most of northcentral USA from Montana to New York and south to Oklahoma and northern Alabama.

# Tadpole madtom
*Noturus gyrinus*

4in (10cm)

**Identification** Uniformly colored, terminal mouth, very small eyes. Pectoral spines smooth, lacks serrations. Upper and lower jaws nearly equal. Four pairs of barbels. Adipose fin continuous with caudal fin.
**Habitat** Quiet areas of small streams, oxbows, sloughs, ponds and sluggish rivers over mud or debris substrates and aquatic vegetation.
**Range** Quebec west to Manitoba, Great Lakes tributaries, east coast from New York to Florida, Mississippi River system to Texas.

# Margined madtom
*Noturus insignis*

5in (13cm)

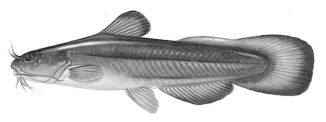

**Identification** Elongate; flattened head, fins having blackish margins, pectoral spine with numerous distinct posterior serrae (nine) and upper jaw extending beyond lower jaw. Adipose fin broadly united to caudal fin.
**Habitat** Clear streams of moderate current in riffles of gravel and rubble.
**Range** Lake Ontario drainage; Atlantic coastal rivers from New York to Georgia; Upper Ohio River and Tennessee River.

# Speckled madtom
*Noturus leptacanthus*

3½in (9cm)

**Identification** Overhanging upper jaw; four pairs of barbels, narrow head. Brownish-yellow sides. Median fins with scattered blackish blotches. Pectoral fin without serrations. Adipose fin continuous with caudal fin.
**Habitat** Small streams with sand or gravel bottoms occurring in debris or vegetation.
**Range** South Carolina west to Tennessee, south to Florida, west to Mississippi and Louisiana

# Brindled madtom
*Noturus miurus*

3½in (9cm)

**Identification** Conspicuously banded and mottled madtom; pectoral spine with large, recurved posterior serrae; four dark saddles crossing dorsum. Black blotch in distal third of dorsal fin; black blotch on adipose fin extending from base to margin. Dusky bands at caudal base and neat margin at caudal fin.
**Habitat** Pools of low to moderate-gradient streams with mud, sand or fine gravel substrates littered with detritus.
**Range** From New York through the Ohio River basin to the lower half of the Mississippi River Valley south to eastern Oklahoma and Mississippi

# Freckled madtom
*Noturus nocturnus*                                    4½in (11cm)

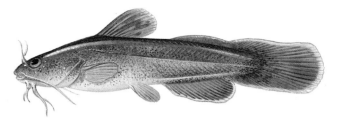

**Identification** Unicolored; low adipose fin barely notched; upper jaw projecting beyond lower. Underparts with fine speckles of dark pigment. Bases of median fins dusky.
**Habitat** Low to moderate gradient, medium to small-sized streams with moderate current over gravel and sand bottoms.
**Range** Central and lower Mississippi valley and several rivers along the Gulf Coast from Alabama to Texas.

# Flathead catfish
*Pylodictis olivaris*                                  53in (1.3m)

**Identification** Mottled; broadly flattened head, projecting lower jaw and slightly notched caudal fin (not forked). Upper lobe of caudal fin depigmented. Adipose fin free. Maximum size about 94lbs (422.6kg).
**Habitat** Deep pools or large streams, rivers and reservoirs adjacent to strong current, usually near rocks, logs, or other debris.
**Range** Southeastern Mississippi River basin north to the Dakotas and Pennsylvania west to Texas and northern Mexico; east in Gulf drainages to Mobile Bay drainage.

# Cavefishes – Amblyopsidae

The cavefish family contains six species, some of which live in caves and others in surface waters. Members are characterized by a usually pale body color, bodies which appear scaleless (although scales are embedded or minute), naked flattened heads, pelvic fins absent or present, anus near the throat (jugular), and many papillose sensory structures on their heads and bodies.

### Ozark cavefish
*Amblyopsis rosae*                                   3in (7.6cm)

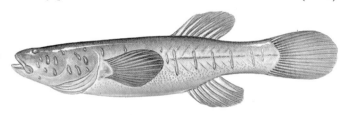

**Identification** Eyeless, depigmented. Pelvic fins absent. Sensory papillae on caudal fin in four to six rows. Anus far in front of anal fin in adults. Skin appears naked (small embedded scales).
**Habitat** Clear pools or slow-moving water of small cave streams.
**Range** Ozark Mountains region of Missouri, Kansas, Oklahoma and Arkansas.

# Northern cavefish
*Amblyopsis spelaea*                                    5in (13cm)

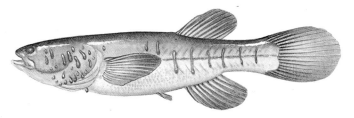

**Identification** Colorless; rudimentary eyes or eyes absent, pelvic fins
extremely small, sensory ridges on head and body. Sensory papillae in
two to three rows on each half of caudal fin. Anus in throat region.
Head naked. Scales on body minute or imbedded.
**Habitat** Subterranean cave streams.
**Range** Southern Indiana; Mammoth Cave region, Kentucky.

# Spring cavefish
*Chologaster agassizi*                                  3in (7.6cm)

**Identification** Elongate; very small eyes. No pelvic fins. Median fins
dusky. Head and body with short rows of sensory papillae. Faint
lateral stripe and basicaudal bar. Scales small and embedded.
**Habitat** Springs and cave streams.
**Range** Kentucky and Tennessee west to Illinois and Missouri.

## Swampfish
*Chologaster cornuta*                                   2in (3cm)

**Identification** Slender; tiny eyes, anus located in throat region, pelvic
fins absent, body without cross ridges or sensory papillae, caudal fin
with a black blotch at base followed by a white blotch or two spots.
**Habitat** Lowland swamps.
**Range** Southern Virginia to central Georgia.


## Southern cavefish
*Typhlichthys subterraneus*                             3in (7.6cm)

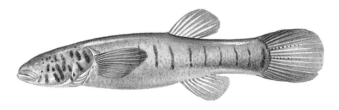

**Identification** Eyeless, unpigmented. Pelvic fins absent. Dorsal and
anal fins far back on the body. Anus in jugular region. Caudal fin
rounded with two rows of sensory papillae, one row in upper half, one
row on lower half.
**Habitat** Pools and quiet waters of small streams of limestone caves
over a rubble or clay bottom.
**Range** Southcentral USA west to the Ozark region of Oklahoma.

# Pirate Perches – Aphredoderidae

The pirate perch is the only species of this North American family. This small species is characterized by ctenoid scales, subthoracic pelvic fins, dorsal fin with three spines and the unique position of the anus under the throat in adults.

## Pirate perch
*Aphredoderus sayanus*                                        5in (13cm)

**Identification** Stout; large mouth; large dorsal fin (three spines, 10–11 rays). Opercle with sharp spine; preopercle serrate. Adipose fin absent. Anus jugular in position. Scales small and strongly ctenoid.
**Habitat** Quiet oxbows, ponds, ditches, swamps, and streams.
**Range** Minnesota south through Mississippi Valley, across Gulf Coast to Florida and north along Atlantic coast to New York.

# Trout Perches – Percopsidae

These small perch-like fishes have an adipose fin and spiny fin rays. Only two species comprise the family.

## Trout-perch
*Percopsis omiscomaycus*                                    6in (15cm)

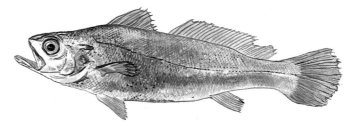

**Identification** Robust; ventral mouth; adipose fin. Body olivaceous to straw colored, rows of dark spots on upper half. Dorsal fin with two to three weak spines and 8–11 soft rays. Lateral line complete with 41–60 scales.
**Habitat** Streams and lakes with sand or gravel bottoms.
**Range** Alaska, Canada, drainages of Hudson and James Bays; Great Lakes and upper Mississippi River system; Connecticut to Maryland.

# Cods – Gadidae

A family of about 60 primarily marine, benthic-dwelling fishes with large heads, wide gill openings, jaws terminal, small cycloid scales, and a slender barbel at the tip of the chin. The burbot is the only truly freshwater species in this family.

## Burbot
*Lota lota*                                                    38in (96cm)

**Identification** Elongate mottled fish; tubular nostrils, single barbel on tip of chin, pelvic fins placed far forward. First dorsal fin short while second dorsal fin long. Anal fin long. Maximum size 18lb 8oz (8.4kg).
**Habitat** Large, cold rivers and lakes.
**Range** Alaska and Canada south to the Missouri and Ohio River drainages.
**Comments** Only exclusively freshwater member of the cod fish family. Spawns in winter under the ice.

# Killifishes – Cyprinodontidae

Members of the killifish family are generally small topwater fishes found in fresh or salt water with dorsoventrally flattened heads, incomplete or partially complete lateral line, and mouths adapted for surface feeding.

## Devil's Hole pupfish
*Cyprinodon diabolis*                                    1¼in (3cm)

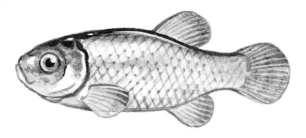

**Identification** Pelvic fins absent; robust terminal mouth. Males iridescent blue with vertical bars on caudal fin; females smaller, more slender, with light spot on their dorsal fin, yellowish brown and no vertical bars on caudal fin.
**Habitat** A single, deep, limestone pool at bottom of Devil's Hole.
**Range** Devil's Hole, Ash Meadows, Neye County, Nevada.

# Desert pupfish
*Cyprinodon macularius*                                    2½in (6.4cm)

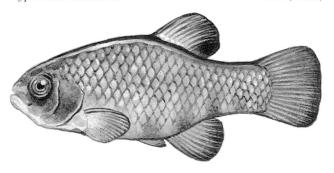

**Identification** Robust; single series of tricuspid teeth. Silvery sides
with six to nine faint bars forming an irregular lateral band. Dorsal fin
(9–12 rays) rounded with a blackish blotch posteriorly.
**Habitat** Desert springs and streams.
**Range** Southern California, Arizona and Northwest Mexico.


# Sheepshead minnow
*Cyprinodon variegatus*                                    3in (7.6cm)

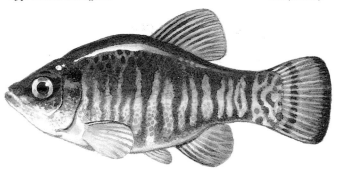

**Identification** Small terminal mouth, tricuspid teeth, and sides with
poorly defined vertical bars. Humeral scale present. Males are an
iridescent blue with a basicaudal bar and caudal fin tipped with black.
Females olivaceous, with black bars on sides and one to two spots on
posterior rays of dorsal fin.
**Habitat** Coastal waters primarily in shallow marshy regions, bayous
and ditches.
**Range** Massachusetts to Northern Mexico.

# Blair's starhead topminnow
*Fundulus blairae*

2in(5cm)

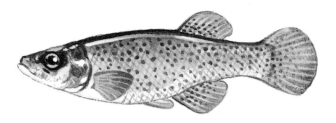

**Identification** Prominent dark bar extending downward below eye; horizontal rows of dots on sides but no vertical bars. Front of dorsal fin base above origin of anal fin base. Lateral line absent, 30–36 scales in series.
**Habitat** Quiet vegetated waters of small streams and vegetated overflow areas of rivers over mud bottoms.
**Range** Gulf drainages from eastern Texas to Alabama north to Oklahoma and Arkansas in Red River system.

# Northern studfish
*Fundulus catenatus*

6in (15cm)

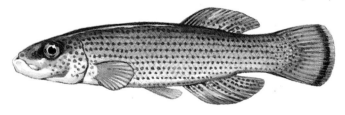

**Identification** Slender; sides with 8–10 thin horizontal lines. Breeding males brightly colored with bright blue sides and reddish-brown streaks. Red spots scattered on sides, operculum and fins. Scales in lateral series 41–49.
**Habitat** Clear, cool streams with moderate gradient over gravel, rock, or sand bottoms.
**Range** Disjunct distribution occurring in Indiana, Virginia to Alabama, Mississippi, Arkansas, Oklahoma and Missouri.

# Golden topminnow
*Fundulus chrysotus*                                   2½in (6.4cm)

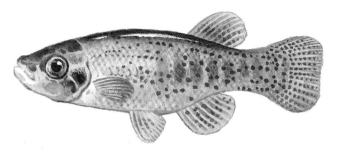

**Identification** Males yellowish green with reddish-brown spots, smaller golden flecks, and dusky vertical bars on sides. Females olive-green with small blue spots on sides, lacking flecks, bars or red spots. Lateral band and suborbital bar absent. Lateral line absent, scales in series 31–35.
**Habitat** Oxbow lakes, sluggish areas of streams and swampy backwater overflows of rivers.
**Range** Atlantic Coast from South Carolina to Florida, west along coast to Texas; Kentucky and southeast Missouri south to Gulf Coast in Mississippi Valley.

# Banded topminnow
*Fundulus diaphanus*                                   3in (7.6cm)

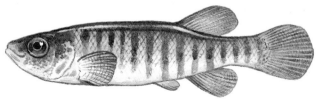

**Identification** Drab-colored; Males with pale or silvery crossbars on sides; females may be plain or with about 15 dark crossbars. Dorsal origin distinctly ahead of anal origin. Scales in lateral series 31–38.
**Habitat** Marine and brackish water of coastal areas.
**Range** Coastal South Carolina to Maritime Province and Newfoundland, west through northern USA and southern Canada to eastern Montana.

# Northern starhead topminnow
*Fundulus dispar*  2½in (6.4cm)

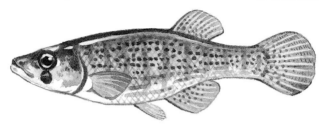

**Identification** Dark, wedge-shaped bar extending downward below
eye and sides with dark vertical bars in males (3–13) and females with
three to six horizontal rows on each side. Lateral line absent with
31–34 scales in series.
**Habitat** Quiet sluggish creeks, oxbow lakes, and vegetated backwater
overflows of rivers.
**Range** Mississippi River Valley from northern Louisiana (Ouachita
River drainage) north to Michigan; upper Mobile Bay drainage,
Alabama.

# Lined topminnow
*Fundulus lineolatus*  2¾in (7cm)

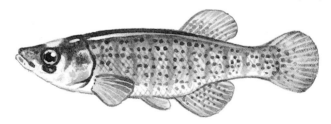

**Identification** Distinct subocular bar, faint longitudinal stripes
formed by dark dots on each scale and 10–12 crossbars, and dorsal fin
origin distinctly behind anal origin. Lateral line absent, with 40–60
scales in series.
**Habitat** Clear streams, backwater regions and lakes.
**Range** Atlantic Coast drainage, southern Virginia south to Florida.

# Blackstripe topminnow
*Fundulus notatus*                                    3in (7.6cm)

**Identification** Wide dark lateral band extending the length of the
body. Spots above lateral band, if present, are few, small, scattered
diffuse and indistinct. Dorsal and caudal fins with dark spots. Lateral
line absent, 31–35 scales in series.
**Habitat** Small to large low-gradient, turbid streams in quiet
backwater areas and pools.
**Range** Lower Mississippi River Valley, north to Iowa.


# Blackspotted topminnow
*Fundulus olivaceus*                                  4in (10cm)

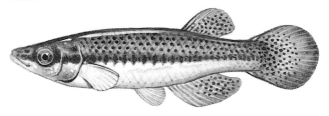

**Identification** Lateral band extending length of body with dark spots
on dorsum and dorsolateral regions. Front of dorsal base situated
posterior to anal fin base. Lateral line absent, 33–37 scales in series.
**Habitat** Streams and rivers over sand and gravel substrates.
**Range** Florida west to Texas and up the lower and middle Mississippi
Valley to Illinois.

## Plains topminnow
*Fundulus sciadicus*

2½in (6.4cm)

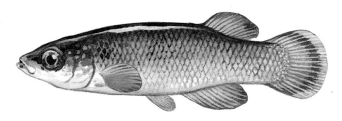

**Identification** Silvery; no lateral band, spots or bars on body. Dorsal fin rays 10–11; origin posterior to anal fin origin. Lateral line absent, 31–39 in lateral series.
**Habitat** Small, weedy springs and spring-fed streams.
**Range** Plains States from Wyoming and South Dakota to Oklahoma and southwest Missouri.


## Longnose killifish
*Fundulus similis*

6in (15cm)

**Identification** Silvery; distinct basicaudal spot. Sides with up to 16 dark vertical bars. Large, black humeral spot present. Dorsal fin origin just anterior to anal fin.
**Habitat** Coastal marshes, tidal pools and ditches over mud and sand substrates.
**Range** Florida to Tampico, Mexico.

# Plains killifish
*Fundulus zebrinus*

5in (13cm)

**Identification** Elongate; caudal margin straight. Body with 15–26 thin, dark vertical bars on sides. Dorsal fin rays 14–15; anal rays 13–14. Dorsal origin anterior to anal fin insertion. Lateral line absent, with 54–63 in lateral series.
**Habitat** Shallow, sandy-bottomed pools, backwaters, and edges of streams and rivers.
**Range** Great Plains east of Rockies from Texas to South Dakota.


# Flagfish
*Jordanella floridae*

2½in (6.4cm)

**Identification** Deep-bodied with a short head; single row of tricuspid teeth. Males with seven to nine reddish-orange stripes along sides and large black blotch below origin of dorsal fin. Dorsal fin rays 16–18 (first fin ray short, thick and spine-like).
**Habitat** Sluggish, vegetated, overflow ditches, ponds and lakes.
**Range** Florida.

# Pygmy killifish
*Leptolucania ommata*

1½in (3.8cm)

**Identification** Slender; five to seven vertical bars on posterior half of body; basicaudal black spot surrounded by a creamy yellow ring at end of black lateral stripe. Body greenish yellow, with a yellowish venter.
**Habitat** Tannin-stained waters of vegetated, sluggish streams, ditches and swamps.
**Range** Georgia south to Florida and west to Mississippi.

# Rainwater killifish
*Lucania parva*

2in (5cm)

**Identification** Small superior mouth with conical teeth; no humeral scale. Sides with margins outlined giving cross-hatched appearance. Lateral stripe present, faint anteriorly, intense on caudal peduncle. Dorsal fin orangish in males with a black spot anteriorly.
**Habitat** Occasionally enters fresh water in bayous; more often estuarine areas.
**Range** Coastal areas from Massachusetts to Mexico. Introduced in California, Nevada, Utah, and Oregon.

# Livebearers – Poeciliidae

The family Poeciliidae is rich in species in tropical and
subtropical areas. As livebearers, females give birth to living
young, unlike most other freshwater fishes in North America.
Males have developed an elongate, copulatory organ called a
gonopodium, for deposition of sperm in the female. Many
species are popular aquarium fishes.

## Mosquitofish
*Gambusia affinis*                                    2¾in (7cm)

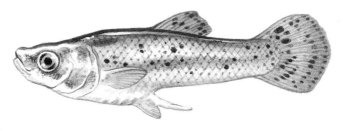

**Identification** Livebearing, top-water species; upturned mouth;
rounded tail. Males with gonopodium. Scales outlined with dark
pigment. Dark suborbital bar and predorsal stripe. Median fins with
flecks of pigment. Females with gravid "spot" near anus.
**Habitat** Swamps, ditches, farm ponds, streams, rivers and lakes.
**Range** Mississippi Valley from Illinois south to Texas, across Gulf
Coast and northward to New Jersey. Widely introduced.

# Least killifish
*Heterandria formosa*

1in (2.5cm)

**Identification** A small, robust killifish with a large eye, terminal
mouth. Sides with six to nine faint bars and lateral stripe ending in
black basicaudal spot. Dorsal and anal fins with basal spots.
Gonopodium in males.
**Habitat** Fresh and brackish water in heavily vegetated bayous,
ditches and swamps.
**Range** North Carolina to Louisiana in coastal drainages.

# Sailfin molly
*Poecilia latipinna*

3in (7.6cm)

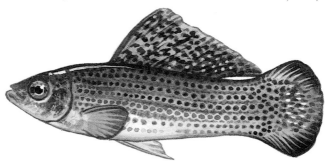

**Identification** An olivaceous-green, slab-sided fish with long,
compressed body, small head, long dorsal fin (14–16 rays) marked
with rows of spots; rounded caudal fin with entire black margin. Body
with horizontal rows of spots, each scale having a spot. Males with
gonopodium.
**Habitat** Bayous and brackish water areas of lowland estuaries,
swamps and streams.
**Range** Coastal form entering fresh water from South Carolina to
Mexico.

# Gila topminnow
*Poeciliopsis occidentalis*                                    2½in (6.4cm)

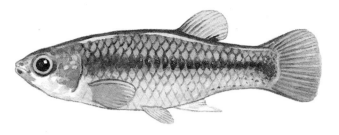

**Identification** Small, superior mouth with lower jaw projecting
slightly. Dorsal fin over anal fin; sides with dark lateral band; no
crossbars. Scales on back darkly outlined, extending as black speckles
to upper belly region. Males with gonopodium. Caudal fin rounded.
**Habitat** Pools of small, sand-bottomed warm-water streams.
**Range** Gila River system, Arizona south to Mexico.

# Silversides – Atherinidae

Silversides are important forage fishes characterized by scaled heads, pectoral fins placed high on the body, no lateral line, two widely separated dorsal fins, a broad, silvery lateral band and the pelvic fins usually abdominal in position.

## Brook silverside
*Labidesthes sicculus*                                   4in (10cm)

**Identification** Elongate; translucent; pointed, beak-like snout; two widely separated dorsal fins. First dorsal with four to five thin, flexible spines; second dorsal with 10–11 rays. Anal fin long, one spine, 20–26 rays.
**Habitat** Calm pools and backwaters of streams, rivers, lakes and reservoirs.
**Range** Throughout most of the eastern states and the Mississippi Valley to Minnesota. Atlantic coastal plain from South Carolina to Florida.

## Inland silverside
*Menidia beryllina*                                      6in (15cm)

**Identification** Elongate; translucent. Flattened head, long anal fin (15–20 rays), two dorsal fins, silvery, lateral band. Snout rounded, shorter than eye. Predorsal scales large, fewer than 23.
**Habitat** Freshwater streams and rivers but entering estuarine along Atlantic and Gulf coasts.
**Range** Along the coast from New England to Mexico in freshwater streams. Lower Mississippi River drainage and Rio Grande.

# Sticklebacks – Gasterosteidae

Sticklebacks are small fishes characterized by slender, streamlined bodies, lacking scales, a series of free dorsal spines anterior to the dorsal fin and pelvic fins reduced to spines.

## Brook stickleback
*Culaea inconstans*                                         3½in (9cm)

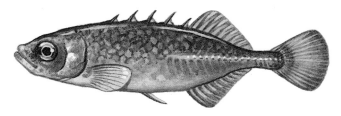

**Identification** Scaleless; four to seven short isolated spines with a backward curve followed by nine to ten soft dorsal rays, rounded caudal fin. Spots or wavy vertical lines on sides.
**Habitat** Cool clear waters.
**Range** Northcentral North America from Nova Scotia and Maine on the east through New York west to Iowa, Montana, north to Hudson Bay drainage and southern Northwest Territories.

# Threespine stickleback
*Gasterosteus aculeatus*                4in (10cm)

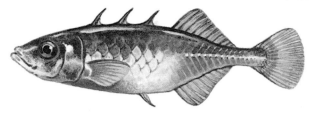

**Identification** A robust, compressed fish with three sharp, free
dorsal spines; scaleless body, series of plates along the sides of the
body.
**Habitat** Marine and freshwater inhabitant; common in nearshore,
vegetated, shallow regions.
**Range** Pacific coast from Baja California north to Alaska; Atlantic
coast from Chesapeake Bay south along coast to western shore of
Hudson Bay, to Baffin Island.


# Ninespine stickleback
*Pungitius pungitius*                2in (5cm)

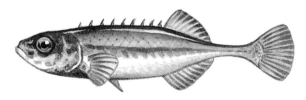

**Identification** A slender, stickleback with 7–12 free dorsal spines;
scaleless body. From 0–15 small bony plates along anterior part of
lateral line.
**Habitat** Lakes and streams; near coastal waters, usually prefers thick
vegetation.
**Range** Circumpolar; in North America, from Alaska north along
coast to Arctic Ocean and east to Atlantic coast, south through
Canada to Indiana and New Jersey.

# Temperate Basses – Moronidae

The temperate bass family in North America is comprised of four popular gamefishes characterized by the presence of two dorsal fins (spines and soft dorsal), large mouth with well-developed teeth, ctenoid scales, sharp spine on operculum, forked caudal fin and pseudobranchiae.

## White perch
*Morone americana*                                                 18in (46cm)

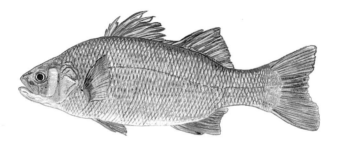

**Identification** Laterally compressed; two dorsal fins slightly joined together at base; lacks stripes on sides. White on belly. No teeth on base of tongue.
**Habitat** Anadromous; rivers and lakes.
**Range** Atlantic coast of North America from St Lawrence River and Gulf of St Lawrence south to South Carolina.
**Comments** Popular game fish on Atlantic coast. Record catch was 4lb 12oz (2.1kg).

# White bass
*Morone chrysops*                                      15in (38cm)

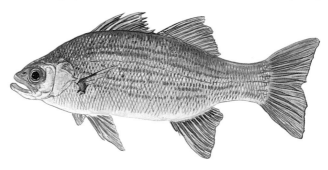

**Identification** A moderately deep-bodied, compressed silver fish with small head, large mouth, six to ten dark, brownish, horizontal stripes on sides. Two separate dorsal fins. Tongue with teeth on back in a single patch. Anal fin with three graduated spines.

**Habitat** Moderate to large clear rivers in current and backwater areas over a firm sand or rock substrate.

**Range** Southern Great Lakes region and Mississippi River valley from Minnesota to Texas and across Gulf states to Florida. Moves into tributaries to spawn in spring.

**Comments** Often called "sandbass" by fishermen, this schooling, open-water fish feeds primarily on small fishes. Weighs up to 5lbs (2.2kg).

# Yellow bass
*Morone mississippiensis* 15in (38cm)

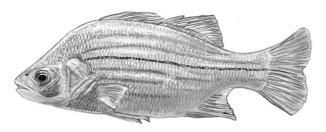

**Identification** Silvery yellow fish with a small head, large mouth, six to eight prominent dark brown or black horizontal stripes on sides, lower stripes sharply broken and offset above the anal fin. First and second dorsal fins slightly connected. Tongue with no teeth on back area.
**Habitat** Clear to turbid backwaters of large rivers and below lakes.
**Range** Mississippi River valley north to Minnesota and Indiana and Gulf coast from Texas to Alabama. Moves into tributary streams in the spring to spawn.
**Comments** Schooling popular game fish. This smaller species has a maximum weight of 1lb (0.5kg).

# Striped bass
*Morone saxatilis* 5ft (1.5m)

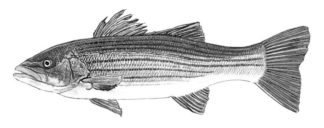

**Identification** A large, streamlined, silver fish with large mouth, seven to eight distinct black horizontal stripes on sides (lower stripes not sharply broken or offset above anal fin origin). Tongue with two parallel patches on back area. Maximum size 59lb 12oz (27.1kg).
**Habitat** Anadromous; marine coastal and estuarine areas; moves into fresh water to spawn.
**Range** Atlantic coast; introduced widely.
**Comments** Popular sport fish. Landlocked freshwater populations developed and stocked widely in reservoirs. World record is 59lb 12oz (27.1kg) for fresh water. In salt water, maximum weight reaches over 100lbs (45kg).

# Sunfishes – Centrarchidae

The sunfish family includes some of the most popular game fishes including the black basses, crappies, rock basses and sunfishes or "bream." Members are characterized by deep, compressed bodies covered with ctenoid scales, spines in the anterior part of the dorsal and anal fins and thoracic pelvic fins.

## Mud sunfish
*Acantharchus pomotis*                                    10in (25cm)

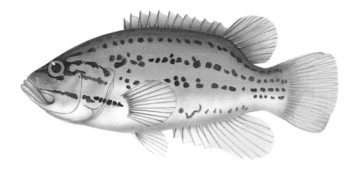

**Identification** Robust, oblong sunfish with three to five irregular greenish-yellow stripes along sides; large mouth (extending past middle of eye). Anal spines 4–6, soft rays 9–12. Caudal fin rounded.
**Habitat** Lowland, tannin-stained, vegetated swamps and streams.
**Range** New York to Florida.

# Shadow bass
*Ambloplites ariommus*                                    8in (20cm)

**Identification** Robust; large eye, four to five wide dark blotches
extending entire width of body, often obscuring horizontal lines on
lower sides. Iris red. Median fins dusky or mottled. Anal rays 5–6.
**Habitat** Clear streams in strong current and heavy aquatic
vegetation.
**Range** Gulf slope drainages from Georgia to eastern Louisiana; lower
Mississippi Valley in Arkansas and Missouri.
**Comments** The shadow bass is a popular game fish.

# Rock bass
*Ambloplites rupestris*                                   13in (33cm)

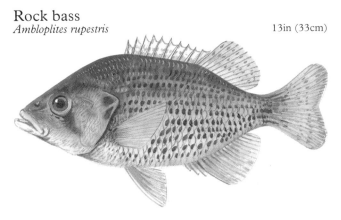

**Identification** Elongate, deep-bodied with a large head, large mouth,
five to six anal spines; red eye. Sides with rows of brown spots and
back with brown or olive mottled with dark blotches.
**Habitat** Small to moderate-sized clear streams and shallow lakes with
vegetation and rocky bottoms.
**Range** Southern Canada (Quebec west to Manitoba); Great Lakes
drainage south to northern Alabama and northern Georgia.
**Comments** A smaller sunfish, the rock bass, is avidly sought by
stream anglers.

# Sacramento perch
*Archoplites interruptus*                                    16in (40cm)

**Identification** Sides mottled with six to eight irregular dark bars.
Anal fin spines 6–7. Preopercle and subopercle serrate.
**Habitat** Sluggish, vegetated streams and lakes.
**Range** California. Introduced elsewhere.
**Comments** The only sunfish native to western USA.


# Flier
*Centrarchus macropterus*                                    8in (20cm)

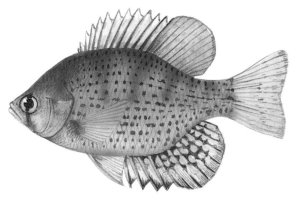

**Identification** Relatively small, deep-bodied, sunfish with the anal
fin almost as long as dorsal fin. Horizontal lines on sides formed by
8–12 conspicuous rows of brown spots. Dark wedge-shaped bar
beneath eye. Young with prominent ocellus in dorsal fin. Anal fin
spines 7 or 8. Maximum weight 1lb (0.5kg).
**Habitat** Quiet oxbow lakes, bayous, creeks and swampy back waters.
**Range** Atlantic coast from Maryland to Florida, west to east Texas;
north through Mississippi Valley to southern Illinois and Indiana.

# Banded pygmy sunfish
*Elassoma zonatum*

2in (5cm)

**Identification** Small, dark, with moderately elongate body, small terminal mouth and rounded caudal fin. Sides with 10–11 brown or black vertical bands and one or two conspicuous black spots below front of dorsal fin. Median fins banded with black. Lateral line absent.
**Habitat** Clear or tannin-stained sluggish streams, bayous, creeks, oxbow lakes and swamps with heavy vegetation over a mud or detritus bottom.
**Range** Mississippi River system from southern Illinois to Texas across Gulf coast to Florida and north to North Carolina on Atlantic coast.

# Bluespotted sunfish
*Enneacanthus gloriosus*

4in (10cm)

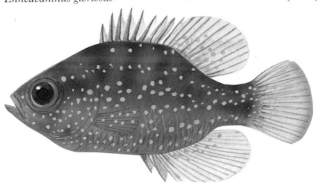

**Identification** Compressed; sides with light blue spots forming longitudinal stripes. Dark spot on upper end of opercle edged with white. Anal fin spines 3. Caudal peduncle scale rows 16–18. Lateral line incompletely developed.
**Habitat** Tannin-stained, sluggish, vegetated streams, swamps, and lakes.
**Range** New York to Florida, west to Mississippi.

# Banded sunfish
*Enneacanthus obesus*

3in (7.6cm)

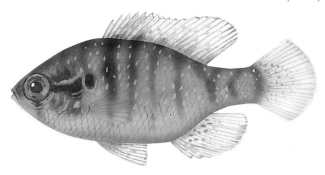

**Identification**  Compressed; five to eight distinct crossbars on sides. Opercular spot as large as eye. Anal spines 3. Caudal fin rounded. Lateral line incompletely developed. Caudal peduncle scale rows 19–22.
**Habitat**  Coastal lowland, vegetated streams, swamps, and lakes.
**Range**  Massachusetts to Florida.


# Redbreast sunfish
*Lepomis auritus*

10in (25cm)

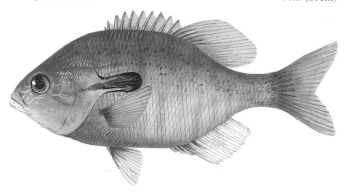

**Identification**  Long, narrow opercular flap, uniformly black to its margin. Pectoral fins short and rounded, 13–15 rays. Anal fin with three spines. Maximum weight 1lb 8oz (0.7kg).
**Habitat**  Streams with slow to moderate current over gravel, rocks, or sand substrates; introduced into ponds and lakes.
**Range**  Eastern coastal streams from New Brunswick south to Florida, west in Gulf coast drainages to Louisiana. Introduced outside native range.

# Green sunfish
*Lepomis cyanellus*

10in (25cm)

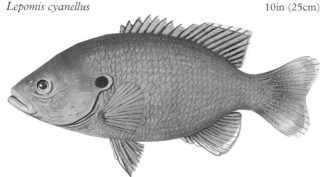

**Identification** Elongate; large mouth. Opercular flap not extended, black with whitish or yellowish-orange margin. Pectoral fin short and rounded. Base of soft dorsal fin and anal fins often with a black spot. Maximum weight about 2lb 4oz (1kg).
**Habitat** Small streams, swamps and ponds.
**Range** Native to southern Great Lakes, Mississippi River basin south to Texas; Alabama west to New Mexico; widely introduced.
**Comments** One of North America's most common sunfishes.

# Pumpkinseed
*Lepomis gibbosus*

10in (25cm)

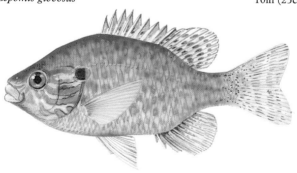

**Identification** Small, compressed sunfish with small head and mouth extending to eye. Opercular flap black bordered by white above and below, red posteriorly. Pectoral fin long, pointed. Dorsal fin spotted and edged in white. Maximum weight about 1lb (0.5kg).
**Habitat** Streams, ponds, and lakes with abundant aquatic vegetation.
**Range** Canada (New Brunswick west to southern Manitoba); Atlantic coast to Georgia; Great Lakes and upper Mississippi River Valley south to southern Illinois. Introduced widely.

# Warmouth
*Lepomis gulosus*

10in (25cm)

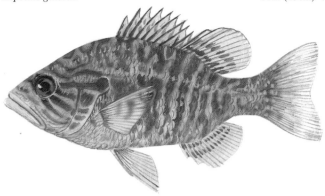

**Identification** Mouth (upper jaw extending beyond middle of red eye), four to five conspicuous lines radiating backward from eye to margin of opercle. Teeth on tongue. Opercular flap short with a black spot. Pectoral fin shot, rounded. Maximum weight 2lb 8oz (1kg).
**Habitat** Ponds and lakes primarily but also inhabits sluggish streams and rivers.
**Range** Most of eastern USA from southern Wisconsin, Michigan and Ohio south through the Mississippi Valley to Texas and the Gulf states.

# Orangespotted sunfish
*Lepomis humilis*

4in (10cm)

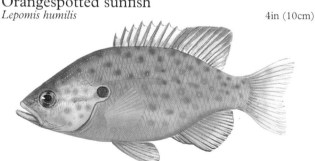

**Identification** Long pectoral fin; orange spots on sides. Opercular flap black and elongated, edge thin and flexible; margin white.
**Habitat** Sluggish, turbid streams, ponds, and lakes over a mud or sand detritus bottom.
**Range** North Dakota east to Ohio southward through the Mississippi basin to Alabama and Louisiana.

# Bluegill
*Lepomis macrochirus*

12in (30cm)

**Identification** Mouth small; long, pointed pectoral fin; black blotch near posterior base of soft dorsal fin. Opercular flap moderately long and black to its margin. Maximum weight 4lb 12oz (2.2kg).
**Habitat** Streams and rivers, lakes, reservoirs and ponds with aquatic vegetation and warm waters.
**Range** From southern Ontario and Quebec through Great Lakes drainage south to Texas and east to Florida. Introduced widely.
**Comments** The bluegill is the most popular freshwater gamefish in the United States. Its widespread occurrence and prolific nature make it an angler's delight.

# Dollar sunfish
*Lepomis marginatus*                                    5in (13cm)

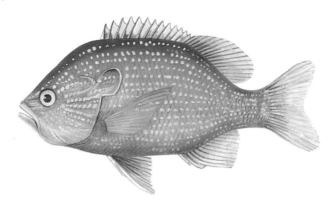

**Identification** Opercular flap elongated with a whitish border. Wavy blue-green lines on cheeks. Pectoral fin short and rounded, with 12 rays. Cheek scales in four rows.
**Habitat** Small sluggish creeks, bayous, and swamps with abundant aquatic vegetation and mud or detritus bottoms.
**Range** Coastal drainages from South Carolina to Texas and north through the Mississippi drainage to Tennessee and Arkansas.

# Longear sunfish
*Lepomis megalotis*                                        7in (18cm)

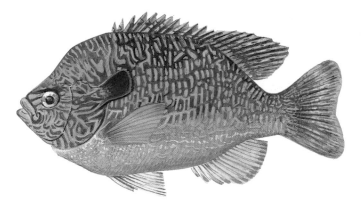

**Identification** Long, flexible, black opercular flap with light border.
Head with alternating orange and blue-green wavy lines. Pectoral fin
short and rounded with 13–15 rays. Cheeks with five to seven scale
rows. Maximum weight about 8oz (226g).
**Habitat** Small, clear upland streams and rivers over gravel and rock
substrates. Also lakes and reservoirs.
**Range** Quebec, Manitoba and western New York in the east
throughout the Mississippi Valley and extending westward through
Minnesota and Nebraska and south into Texas; along Gulf Coast
drainages to west Florida.
**Comments** This very popular gamefish is widespread and avidly
sought by both stream and reservoir fishermen.

# Redear sunfish
*Lepomis microlophus*                                        14in (36cm)

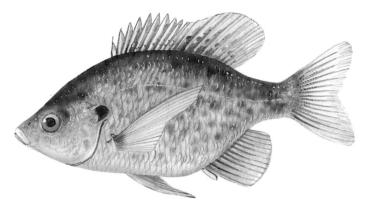

**Identification**  Short opercular flap edged with a bright red posterior crescent. Mouth small. Pectoral fins long and pointed. No black blotch in the posterior rays of dorsal fin. Maximum weight 4lb 8oz (2kg).

**Habitat**  Sluggish streams and rivers, lakes, reservoirs and ponds with an abundance of cover and aquatic vegetation.

**Range**  Mississippi River system from Indiana and Missouri south to the Gulf states and Florida. Widely introduced elsewhere.

**Comments**  In the deep south, this sunfish is called a "shellcracker" or "stumpknocker" because of its penchant for crushing snails with its molar-like teeth.

# Spotted sunfish
*Lepomis punctatus*                                        8in (20cm)

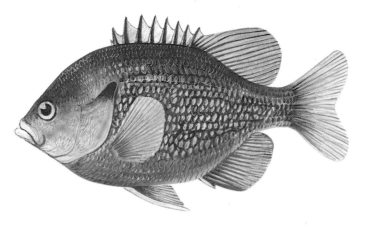

**Identification**  Short, rounded pectoral fin; short, dark opercular flap stiff to its margin. Scales on sides with reddish spots in males, yellow spots in females.
**Habitat**  Streams, rivers and oxbow lakes in quiet clear waters with abundant aquatic vegetation over mud bottoms.
**Range**  Indiana and Missouri through the Mississippi basin to the Gulf states east to North Carolina.

# Smallmouth bass
*Micropterus dolomieui*                                24 in (61cm)

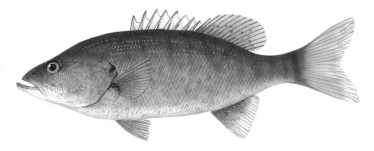

**Identification** Elongate; low spinous dorsal fin joined broadly to the soft-rayed portion. Upper jaw of mouth not extending past rear margin of eye. No lateral band. Body olive-brown to bronze with plain sides.

**Habitat** Cool, clear, rocky and gravel-bottomed streams with moderate to swift current; lakes and reservoirs.

**Range** From Quebec and Ontario and Great Lakes region west to South Dakota and Iowa and south to Oklahoma, Arkansas and northern Alabama.

**Comments** The smallmouth bass is one of the angler's favorites. Fly fishermen and other anglers pursue this delightful fighting fish in mountain streams throughout its range. Maximum weight 12lbs (5.4kg); it has been said the smallmouth is the gamest fish around. It feeds on crayfish, insects and fishes.

# Spotted bass
*Micropterus punctulatus*                                24in (61cm)

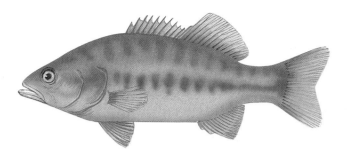

**Identification** Dark blotches forming a longitudinal band on sides; upper jaw of mouth reaching to or slightly behind rear margin of the eye. Lower sides with horizontal rows of dark spots. Dorsal fins fairly broad, joined to the rayed portion of the dorsal. Maximum weight 9lbs (4kg).

**Habitat** Large streams and rivers; also lakes and reservoirs.

**Range** Southcentral USA from Kansas and Texas in the west to Illinois and Pennsylvania in the north and south to Georgia and the Gulf states.

**Comments** Popular game fish taken on live or artificial baits. The spotted bass has adapted well to reservoirs, although it is most abundant in streams and rivers.

# Largemouth bass
*Micropterus salmoides* 38in (96cm)

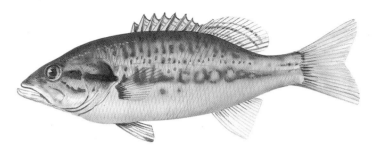

**Identification** Large mouth (upper jaw extends far behind rear margin of eye); midsides with a broad, dark, longitudinal band. Spinous and soft dorsal fins almost separate. Maximum size 22lb 4oz (10 kg).

**Habitat** Highly successful lake, pond and reservoir fish, but does well in deep, quiet pools of large streams and rivers.

**Range** Southern Ontario west to Minnesota and Nebraska, south to the Gulf states, north along the east coast to North Carolina. Widely introduced throughout southern Canada and USA.

**Comments** Arguably the largemouth bass may be the most widely sought fish in the USA. This popular game and sport fish is responsible for "contests" being held in which the winners earn thousands of dollars for catching the largest fish.

# White crappie
*Pomoxis annularis*

15in (38cm)

**Identification** Ten or fewer faint vertical bars on sides. Spinous and soft dorsal fins broadly joined. Dorsal spines 6. Anal spines 6. Median fins mottled with black.

**Habitat** Streams, rivers, ponds, lakes and reservoirs near brush piles or standing timber.

**Range** Southern Ontario west to Minnesota and Nebraska south through the Mississippi basin in Gulf states, north along Atlantic coast to North Carolina.

**Comments** Popular food fish, highly prized for its tasty flesh. Taken on both natural and artificial baits. Wide ecological tolerances.

# Black crappie
*Pomoxis nigromaculatus*

16in (40cm)

**Identification** Median fins mottled with black. Spinous and soft dorsal fins broadly joined. Dorsal fin with seven to eight spines; anal fin with six spines. Maximum weight 5lbs (2.3kg).

**Habitat** Quiet waters of streams, ponds, lakes and reservoirs almost always near brush piles.

**Range** Quebec, Ontario, and southern Manitoba; eastern USA south to Texas and Florida except Atlantic coast streams. Widely introduced.

**Comments** Popular sport and food fish prized for the flavor of its flesh. Not as abundant or tolerant of turbidity as the white crappie.

# Darters and Perches – Percidae

Three subgroups comprise this large family of about 150
North American species: (1) walleye and sauger, (2) perch,
and (3) darters. Members of this family are characterized by
ctenoid scales, two distinct dorsal fins, pelvic fins thoracic in
position, and one or two anal spines.

## Yellow perch
*Perca flavescens*                                    15in (38cm)

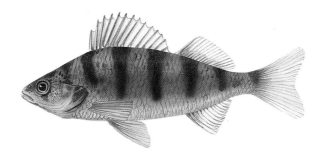

**Identification**  Two separate dorsal fins; large mouth; no canine
teeth. Six to eight dusky vertical bars on back and sides. Posterior base
of first dorsal fin with dark spot. Preopercle serrate. Anal fin with two
spines.
**Habitat**  Large clear streams, lakes and reservoirs with aquatic
vegetation.
**Range**  Eastern Canada, south along the Atlantic coast to Florida,
and through the upper Mississippi River system south to Kansas.
Introduced elsewhere.
**Comments**  Important as a sport and food fish, the yellow perch is
harvested commercially in Canada and the Great Lakes region. Live
bait is preferred by fishermen.

# Sauger
*Stizostedion canadense*

28in (71cm)

**Identification**  Elongate; mouth large with canine teeth; two separate dorsal fins; three to four dark saddles extending obliquely forward to middle of sides. First dorsal with black spots. No black blotch at posterior end of first dorsal. Anal spines 2. Preopercle serrate.
**Habitat**  Moderate to large streams and rivers with moderate to swift current; lakes and reservoirs.
**Range**  Quebec to Alberta; St Lawrence River to Great Lakes west to Montana south through Mississippi River system to Oklahoma, Arkansas, Alabama and Tennessee. Introduced outside native range.
**Comments**  In Canada this popular sport and food fish is harvested commercially. Feeds mainly on fishes. Maximum life span is seven years.

# Walleye
*Stizostedion vitreum*

41in (1m)

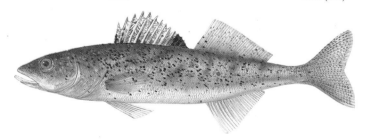

**Identification**  Streamlined; large mouth with canine teeth; two separate dorsal fins. Black blotch on the posterior membranes of spinous dorsal fin. Preopercle serrate.
**Habitat**  Large streams, rivers, lakes and reservoirs in deep areas over sand, gravel or rock substrates.
**Range**  Southern Hudson Bay drainage west to Mackenzie River in Canada; south through Great Lakes and Mississippi River system to Louisiana, east to Alabama.
**Comments**  This highly prized sport and food fish is the largest North American perch member. It feeds on fishes and a variety of aquatic invertebrates. Widely stocked in reservoirs.

# Crystal darter
*Ammocrypta asprella*                                    4in (10cm)

**Identification** Slender; large eyes, four dark, wide dorsal saddles extending obliquely forward and with a midlateral series of oblong dark blotches. Body fully scaled.
**Habitat** Moderate-sized rivers in strong current over a sand or fine gravel substrate.
**Range** Mississippi River system from Minnesota, Ohio and West Virginia south to Louisiana; Gulf Coast drainages from west Florida to Louisiana.


# Western sand darter
*Ammocrypta clara*                                    2¼in (5.8cm)

**Identification** Thin midlateral stripe. Nine to eleven dark elongate blotches on sides. Opercular spine present. Three to five rows of scales along sides.
**Habitat** Moderate-sized rivers in slight to moderate current over a sandy bottom.
**Range** Generally west of the Mississippi River; Ohio River drainage in Indiana, Kentucky; Mississippi River system from southern Minnesota south to Mississippi, Arkansas and east Texas; Ohio River drainage in Tennessee, Kentucky and Indiana.

# Eastern sand darter
*Ammocrypta pellucida*                    2½in (6.4cm)

**Identification** Round, dark spots just below lateral line, 11–15.
Opercular spine absent. Scale rows above lateral line 1–4, 4–7 rows
below. Soft dorsal fin without a dusky bar at base.
**Habitat** Moderate-sized streams and rivers with moderate current
over clean sand substrates.
**Range** East of the Mississippi basin from southern Illinois and
Kentucky through the Mississippi, Ohio, and Great Lakes drainages to
southern Michigan and Ontario.

# Scaly sand darter
*Ammocypta vivax*                         2½in (6.4cm)

**Identification** Opercular spine present. More than five rows of scales
on the sides. Nape scaled. Nine to 16 midlateral dark, oval blotches
vertically oriented. Body mostly scaled.
**Habitat** Moderate-sized streams and rivers in moderate current over
clean sand.
**Range** Mississippi River system from Mississippi to Texas and north
into Oklahoma, Missouri and western Kentucky.

# Mud darter
*Etheostoma asprigene*                                    2½in (6.4cm)

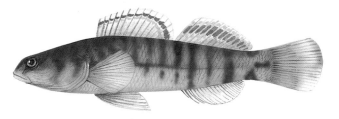

**Identification** Six to eight vertical bars (five to six posterior bars distinct) on caudal peduncle; eight to nine dorsal saddles. Cheek, opercle and nape fully scaled. Lateral line incomplete with 44–54 in lateral series (31–44 pored).
**Habitat** Sluggish streams and bayous over mud and sand bottoms.
**Range** Mississippi basin from Minnesota to the Gulf states.


# Greenside darter
*Etheostoma blennioides*                                  6in (15cm)

**Identification** Blunt snout overhangs inferior mouth. Skin over maxilla fused with skin of snout. Sides with five to eight dark V- or W-shaped blotches. Dorsum with five to eight dark saddles and red spots.
**Habitat** Small creeks and moderate-sized streams and rivers with moderate to swift current, low turbidity over gravel riffles.
**Range** From southern Ontario, and Great Lakes region (New York and Michigan) throughout the Ohio and Tennessee systems, south and west to Arkansas, Oklahoma and Kansas.

# Rainbow darter
*Etheostoma caeruleum*                                     3in (7.6cm)

**Identification**  Body deepest under first dorsal fin. Eight to 11 blue-green vertical bars alternating with wider orange spaces on sides. Anal fin with blue and red. Lateral line incomplete; 16–39 pored scales.
**Habitat**  Swift, gravel riffles of clear, cool creeks, and small rivers.
**Range**  Southern Ontario, from New York west to southern Minnesota, south to northern Alabama and northern Arkansas. Also in southwest Mississippi and eastern Louisiana.

# Bluebreast darter
*Etheostoma camurum*                                       3in (7.6cm)

**Identification**  Large and robust with nine to 14 horizontal dark stripes on sides. Body dark with red spots on sides. Humeral spot conspicuous. Midlateral spot at caudal base divided and flanked above and below with creamy-colored areas.
**Habitat**  Medium-sized to large rivers in swift riffles over coarse gravel, rubble and boulder substrates.
**Range**  Ohio River basin from Pennsylvania to Illinois and south to Tennessee, Virginia, and North Carolina.

# Bluntnose darter
*Etheostoma chlorosomum*                              2in (5cm)

**Identification** Straw-colored; blunt snout; X- or W-shaped markings on sides. Preorbital bar dark extending onto snout and fusing opposite side. Cheeks partially scaled. Lateral line incomplete. Anal spine, 1.
**Habitat** Sluggish streams, bayous, swamps, and oxbow lakes in quiet water over sand, mud or detritus bottoms.
**Range** Central Mississippi Valley from Minnesota to Texas and along Gulf Coast to Alabama.

# Creole darter
*Etheostoma collettei*                              2½in (6.4cm)

**Identification** Small darter with eight to nine dorsal saddles, four darker than the others; five to seven vertical bars developed posteriorly on caudal peduncle. Opercle scaled. Lower half of cheek scaled. Lateral line incomplete.
**Habitat** Headwater creeks and small rivers in swift current over a gravel bottom.
**Range** Ouachita and Little River systems, Arkansas and Louisiana; Little, Red, and Sabine drainage of Louisiana.

# Arkansas darter
*Etheostoma cragini*                                    2in (5cm)

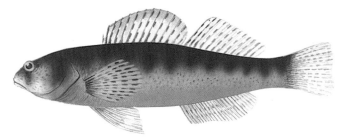

**Identification**  Body bicolored; body and head thickly stippled with black spots. Dorsum crossed by six to nine small saddles. Sides with nine to 12 dusky blotches. Suborbital bar distinct. Lateral line incomplete. Scales pored, 12–20.
**Habitat**  Small permanent springs and spring-fed creeks which are heavily vegetated.
**Range**  Arkansas River system in Colorado, Kansas, Oklahoma, and Arkansas.

# Arkansas saddled darter
*Etheostoma euzonum*                                    4½in (11cm)

**Identification**  Robust, olive-tan darter with four broad dark saddles crossing dorsum and extending obliquely forward. Sides may be mottled with small orange and green spots. Gill membranes broadly connected. Lateral line complete, 54–71 scales.
**Habitat**  Deep, swift riffles of large clear upland streams and rivers.
**Range**  White River drainage in Ozark Uplands of Arkansas and Missouri.

# Iowa darter
*Etheostoma exile*                                    3in (7.6cm)

**Identification** Slender darter with large eye, 10–12 dark, squarish, midlateral blotches on sides with dark red between. Dorsal fins separate. Lateral line incomplete. Caudal peduncle long and slender.
**Habitat** Quiet vegetated areas of streams and lakes over mud and sand substrates.
**Range** Quebec to Alberta; New York west Montana, south to Ohio, and west to Wyoming and Colorado.

# Fantail darter
*Etheostoma flabellare*                               3in (7.6cm)

**Identification** Each lateral scale with small black spot, causing horizontal stripes. Gill membranes broadly connected. First dorsal fin very low. Tips of spines of first dorsal fin with fleshy knob in males. Lateral line incomplete, 15–16 pored scales.
**Habitat** Clear, small streams and spring-fed creeks in swift, shallow riffles over gravel and rubble bottoms.
**Range** Southwest Quebec and southeastern Ontario; from New York west to Minnesota and south to North Carolina, Alabama, Arkansas, Oklahoma and Louisiana.

# Swamp darter
*Etheostoma fusiforme*                                    2in (5cm)

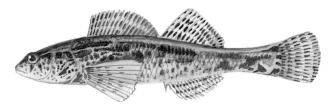

**Identification** Small, elongate darter with small head and nine to 12
midlateral blotches; frenum present. Lower side often spotted or
stippled. Caudal fin barred; base with four dark spots. Breast and top
of head scaled. Lateral line highly arched, incomplete, 11–27 pored
scales.
**Habitat** Vegetated, backwater areas of lowland streams, swamps and
oxbow lakes over mud or sand substrates.
**Range** Coastal streams from North Carolina to Louisiana and north
in the Mississippi River system to Oklahoma, Arkansas, and
Tennessee.

# Slough darter
*Etheostoma gracile*                                      2in (5cm)

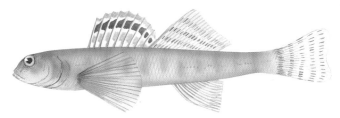

**Identification** Slender darter with small head and highly arched
lateral line anteriorly. Sides with eight to ten blotches or bars (males
with bright green vertical bars). Cheek and opercle fully scaled.
Lateral line incomplete, 16–23 pored. Breast and top of head naked.
**Habitat** Quiet backwater areas of sluggish bayous, creeks, oxbow
lakes, ditches and lakes.
**Range** Southern Illinois through the lower Mississippi basin to
Oklahoma and Louisiana and coastal streams in eastern Texas.

# Harlequin darter
*Etheostoma histrio*                                    3in (7.6cm)

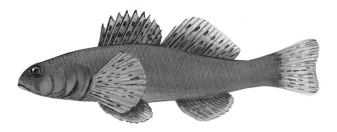

**Identification** Large expansive pectoral fins. Body with six to seven dark brown or green dorsal saddles and seven to 11 dark vertical bars on sides. All fins with dark spots. Lateral line complete with 45–58 scales.
**Habitat** Large streams and small to moderate-sized rivers in swift gravel riffles.
**Range** Southern Indiana to Alabama and western Florida in the east, Oklahoma and Texas in the west, and Louisiana and Mississippi in the south.

# Spotted darter
*Etheostoma maculatum*                                  3in (7.6cm)

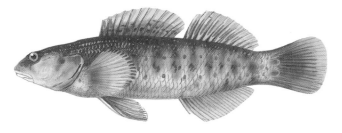

**Identification** Deep caudal peduncle. Scales with a pattern of narrow longitudinal, dark lines made up of dusky spots (males with bright red spots). Gill membranes narrowly joined. Lateral line usually complete with 57–62 scales.
**Habitat** Large, clear, cold streams and rivers over rubble and rock substrates in swift sections.
**Range** New York west to Indiana, south to Tennessee and North Carolina.

# Least darter
*Etheostoma microperca*                                    1½in (3.8cm)

**Identification** A tiny darter with seven to ten small dark blotches on sides. Gill membranes broadly joined across throat. Lateral line absent to with one or two pored scales.
**Habitat** Clear springs or small spring-fed streams having gravel bottoms and watercress.
**Range** Lower Great Lakes and upper Mississippi drainages from Minnesota and Ohio south and west to Oklahoma.


# Johnny darter
*Etheostoma nigrum*                                        2½in (6.4cm)

**Identification** Small, slender straw-colored darter, with eight or nine W-shaped lateral blotches. Anal fin with one spine. Lateral line complete with 40–55 scales. Preorbital dark bars not continuous on snout.
**Habitat** Streams and small rivers in pools with sand or gravel bottoms.
**Range** Quebec and southern Hudson Bay drainage to Saskatchewan; most of northeastern and northcentral USA from the Great Lakes to Louisiana and from Georgia to Oklahoma.

# Tessellated darter
*Etheostoma olmstedi*                                  3½in (9cm)

**Identification** Small, elongate, darter with nine to 11 X- or W-shaped markings on sides. Dorsum crossed by six dark saddles. Anal fin spines 1–2. Lateral line complete with 37–58 scales.
**Habitat** Sluggish streams over sand, mud or gravel substrates; also near lake shores.
**Range** Quebec and Ontario (St Lawrence and Lake Ontario drainages) Atlantic Coast drainages south to Florida.

# Cypress darter
*Etheostoma proeliare*                                  2in (5cm)

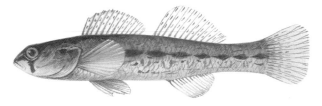

**Identification** Short lateral line (two to seven pored scales). Seven to 12 dark brown lateral blotches. Sides with numerous small brown spots. Dusky mottling on dorsal and caudal fins.
**Habitat** Small streams, bayous, oxbow lakes, and swamps with little or no current over mud and detritus bottoms, often in aquatic vegetation.
**Range** Illinois and Missouri south to Texas and western Florida.

## Stippled darter
*Etheostoma punctulatum*                3½in (9cm)

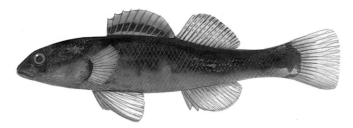

**Identification** Four conspicuous dark saddles on back, sides with midlateral blue-green band posteriorly and undersides sprinkled with conspicuous spots. All fins spotted or barred. Lateral line incomplete, 58–80 scales in lateral series. Broad black bar beneath eye.
**Habitat** Clear, cool creeks or spring brooks with vegetation and gravel or rock substrates.
**Range** Southeastern Kansas, southwestern Missouri, northeastern Oklahoma and northern Arkansas.

## Redline darter
*Etheostoma rufilineatum*                3½in (9cm)

**Identification** Sides of males marked with longitudinal lines and various color dashes (red, orange, green). Creamy areas in upper and lower base of caudal fin. Lateral line complete, 41–57 scales.
**Habitat** Clear, cold streams and rivers in swift, gravel riffles and rock substrates.
**Range** Cumberland and Tennessee River drainages of Virginia, Kentucky, Georgia and Alabama.

# Tennessee snubnose darter
*Etheostoma simoterum*                    3in (7.6cm)

**Identification** Snout blunt; strongly decurved. Sides with series of
dark blotches forming irregular lateral band. Dorsolateral area tan
with reddish scales sometimes forming zigzag lines. Frenum narrow.
Pectoral fin rays 14.
**Habitat** Streams and small rivers over shallow gravel riffles.
**Range** Virginia to North Carolina south to Alabama.

# Orangethroat darter
*Etheostoma spectabile*                    2½in (6.4cm)

**Identification** Greatest body depth just in front of first dorsal fin.
Sides with eight to 11 blue-green lateral bands, alternating with red-
orange areas. Anal fin blue-green. Lateral line incomplete, 15–20
pored scales.
**Habitat** Gravel riffles in small to moderate-sized streams.
**Range** From Michigan west to Colorado and south to Texas,
Arkansas and Tennessee.

# Spotted darter
*Etheostoma squamiceps*                                      3in (7.6cm)

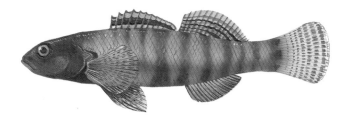

**Identification** Low spiny dorsal fin; interrupted supratemporal and infraorbital canals. Upper sides stippled, mottled, or covered with zigzag lines. Distinct basicaudal spot, flanked by two smaller spots. Caudal fin with vertical bands.
**Habitat** Small to medium-sized streams of low to moderate gradient in quiet pools under rocks, vegetation, and debris.
**Range** Lower Tennessee River, Green River and tributaries to Ohio River.

# Speckled darter
*Etheostoma stigmaeum*                                       2in (5cm)

**Identification** Straw-colored, with five to seven dorsal saddles; eight to ten lateral blotches. No frenum. Preorbital dark bar extending onto snout, not continuous around snout. Lateral line incomplete, 27–34 pored.
**Habitat** Pools and riffles in clear, small to medium-sized streams having moderate current over sand, gravel or rock substrates.
**Range** From Kansas and Oklahoma east to Kentucky and western Florida and south to Louisiana and Texas.

# Gulf darter
*Etheostoma swaini*                                     2½in (6.4cm)

**Identification** Small, brownish darter with seven to nine dorsal saddles; sides with spots on the scales creating well-defined longitudinal stripes. Caudal peduncle with four to eight poorly defined bars. Two circular unpigmented basicaudal spots. Lateral line complete or nearly so with up to seven unpored scales.
**Habitat** Streams and small rivers over sand or gravel substrates.
**Range** Kentucky and Tennessee south to Georgia and Florida, west to Louisiana.

# Redfin darter
*Etheostoma whipplei*                                   3½in (9cm)

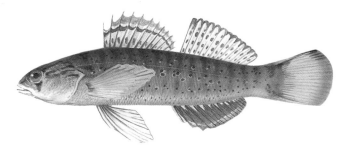

**Identification** Frenum present. Eight to ten small saddles across dorsum. Sides mottled with six to nine dark blotches. Males with red spots. Three basicaudal spots. Scales small, 57–70 in lateral series.
**Habitat** Small to medium-sized streams of high gradient in gravel-bottomed riffles.
**Range** Arkansas River system in eastern Oklahoma and Kansas and western Missouri, east Texas and Arkansas.

# Banded darter
*Etheostoma zonale*

3in (7.6cm)

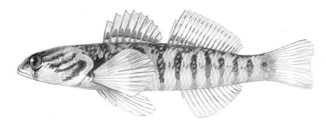

**Identification** Blunt snout; nine to 13 dark green lateral blotches and vertical bars. Base of caudal fin with vertical row of three or four small, dark spots. Gill membranes broadly connected. Lateral line scales 46–63.
**Habitat** Moderate-sized streams and rivers of moderate to swift current over deep gravel and rubble riffles.
**Range** From Pennsylvania west to Minnesota and south to Georgia and Louisiana.

# Backwater darter
*Etheostoma zoniferum*

1½in (3.8cm)

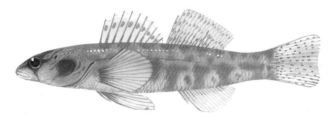

**Identification** Highly arched, incomplete lateral line (13–19 pores); eight to ten lateral blotches; eight to 11 indistinct dorsal saddles. Cheeks and opercle scaled.
**Habitat** Pools of small streams of slow to moderate current over sand and silt substrates.
**Range** Tombigbee and Mobile drainage of Mississippi and Alabama.

# Tangerine darter
*Percina aurantiaca*                                          5in (13cm)

**Identification** One of the most beautiful darters, this large robust darter has 84–95 lateral line scales; a series of dusky spots along upper sides. Eight to ten large blotches in dark lateral band. Lower sides suffused with orange in breeding males. Basicaudal spot.
**Habitat** Rivers of moderate to steep gradient in current and deeper areas around boulders.
**Range** Tennessee River drainage of Tennessee, North Carolina, Georgia, and Virginia.


# Logperch
*Percina caprodes*                                           7in (18cm)

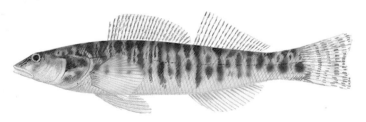

**Identification** Conical head; pointed snout; 15–20 dark vertical bars along side. Basicaudal spot. Dorsum with 15–22 dark saddles.
**Habitat** Pools and deep riffles of moderate to large streams and rivers; also found in lakes and reservoirs.
**Range** Southern Canada through the Great Lakes to the Mississippi River system south to Texas, Louisiana, and east to west Florida.

# Channel darter
*Percina copelandi*

2½in (6.4cm)

**Identification** Blunt snout; no frenum; nine to 12 dark oblong blotches along the undersides. Black preorbital bar present. One or more enlarged and modified scales between pelvic bases. Lateral line complete with 51–60 scales.
**Habitat** Small to moderate-sized rivers in riffles of moderate swift current over gravel and rock bottoms.
**Range** Upper St Lawrence basin through Ohio and southern Michigan south through Ohio basin to Alabama River system and Red River system of Oklahoma.

# Gilt darter
*Percina evides*

3½in (9cm)

**Identification** Stout-bodied, with series of seven to nine dark blotches along the midsides, each blotch directly below a dorsal saddle. Frenum present. Lateral line complete, 64–76 scales.
**Habitat** Large streams and small to medium-sized rivers over clean gravel and rubble substrates in swift current.
**Range** From New York to Mississippi River system in Wisconsin and Minnesota, south to Georgia, Alabama and Arkansas.

## Freckled darter
*Percina lenticula*                                    6½in (16.5cm)

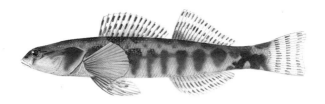

**Identification** Three vertically arranged caudal spots (lower two sometimes fused); small scales (lateral line scales 80–86). Eight dark blotches surrounded by a pale area on dorsum; eight dark lateral blotches often connected by a lateral band. Fins boldly patterned.
**Habitat** Medium to large-sized rivers in deep swift water.
**Range** Mobile basin of Georgia and Alabama; Pearl and Pascagoula drainages of Mississippi and Louisiana.

## Blackside darter
*Percina maculata*                                     4½in (11cm)

**Identification** Moderately slender darter with six to nine oval dark blotches along midside; suborbital bar; basicaudal spot. Eight to nine dusky saddles on dorsum. Gill membranes separate. Lateral line complete, 62–79 scales.
**Habitat** Pools and riffles of slow to moderate current over gravel or rock substrates in large streams and rivers.
**Range** From Ontario to Manitoba and Saskatchewan through the southern Great Lakes and Mississippi River system; Gulf Coast drainages from Texas to Alabama.

# Longnose darter
*Percina nasuta*                                   4in (10cm)

**Identification** Extremely long, pointed snout; 12–15 dark blotches
or vertically elongated bars on midsides. Basicaudal spot. Six or seven
branchiostegal rays. Lateral line complete, 65–83 scales.
**Habitat** Clear, silt-free upland streams and small rivers with gravel or
cobblestone bottoms.
**Range** Ozark Uplands of Missouri, Arkansas, and Oklahoma.

# Blackbanded darter
*Percina nigrofasciata*                            5in (13cm)

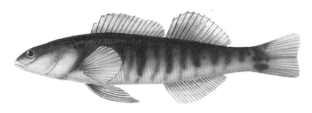

**Identification** Moderately large; short, pointed snout and 11–13
elongate or elliptical black vertical bars on sides, three dark basicaudal
spots. Frenum present. Gill membranes slightly connected. Lateral
line complete, 50–64 scales.
**Habitat** Lowland streams and small rivers with moderate current
over sand substrates and gravel riffles.
**Range** South Carolina to Florida, west to Louisiana.

# Yellow darter
*Percina ouachitae* 2½in (6.4cm)

**Identification** Five dorsal saddles, first saddle beneath first dorsal fin, last saddles over end of caudal peduncle and usually indistinct. Eight to ten brown or black lateral blotches. Cross-hatching on upper sides. Lateral line complete, 48–62 scales.
**Habitat** Moderate-sized rivers in shallow to medium-sized riffles over fine gravel or sand bottom.
**Range** Gulf Slope from western Florida to Louisiana north in Mississippi Valley to Missouri and Kentucky.

# Shield darter
*Percina peltata* 2½in (6.4cm)

**Identification** Olivaceous darter with six to eight squarish lateral blotches on sides; dorsum with eight saddles. Caudal spot present. Well-developed suborbital bar. Caudal fin with four vertical bands. Lateral line with 52–61 scales.
**Habitat** Rivers and moderate-sized streams in riffles.
**Range** Atlantic Coast streams from Hudson River south to North Carolina.

## Slenderhead darter
*Percina phoxocephala*                                      4in (10cm)

**Identification**  Moderately long, pointed snout. Small basicaudal spot. Midsides with 10–15 dark round to square blotches, anterior blotches generally larger and slimmer. Six branchiostegal rays. Lateral line complete, 61–73 scales.
**Habitat**  Gravel and rocky riffles of moderate to large-sized streams and rivers.
**Range**  Central Ohio and Mississippi basins, from Minnesota to Pennsylvania, south to Oklahoma and Tennessee.

## Dusky darter
*Percina sciera*                                            4½in (11cm)

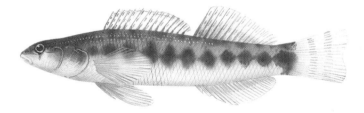

**Identification**  Eight to ten midlateral dark blotches which tend to be connected by lateral band. Caudal base with three round black spots, lower two usually connected. Gill membranes broadly connected. Edge of preopercle often serrate.
**Habitat**  Small streams and small to medium-sized low gradient rivers in riffles in slow to moderate current over gravel or detritus bottoms.
**Range**  Lower Ohio and Mississippi drainages from Ohio through Tennessee and Missouri south to Texas and Alabama.

# River darter
*Percina shumardi*                                            3½in (9cm)

**Identification** Eight to 13 dark blotches on midsides, two
conspicuous black blotches in spinous dorsal fin, black suborbital bar,
and anal fin of male greatly elongated. Small basicaudal spot.
**Habitat** Larger rivers and lower reaches of moderate-sized lowland
rivers in swift current over gravel or sand bottoms.
**Range** Southern Manitoba through parts of the Great Lakes and
Ohio drainages, south through the Mississippi basin to Alabama and
Texas.


# Snail darter
*Percina tanasi*                                             3in (7.6cm)

**Identification** Snout decurved, mouth horizontal; four broad, dark
saddles crossing dorsum and extending to the lateral line. First band
beneath anterior dorsal fin spines. Sides with midlateral blotches.
**Habitat** Medium to large-sized streams over clean, shoal areas and
gravel riffles.
**Range** Tennessee River drainage of Tennessee, Alabama and
Georgia.

# Stargazing darter
*Percina uranidea*

3½in (9cm)

**Identification** Four distinct saddles crossing dorsum, the fourth saddle located over the dorsal insertion of caudal fin. Saddles extending downward, connected to a row of nine to 12 vertically oblong dark blotches on sides.
**Habitat** Moderate-sized rivers in swift current of deep gravel riffles.
**Range** Ouachita River system of Arkansas and Louisiana; White River system of northeastern Arkansas and southern Missouri.

# Drums – Sciaenidae

Although mostly marine, one species, the freshwater drum, is confined to fresh water and is characterized by a deep, silvery body with the lateral line extending onto the caudal fin.

## Freshwater drum
*Aplodinotus grunniens*                                    35in (89cm)

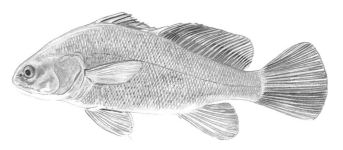

**Identification** A large, silvery or gray fish with a highly developed lateral line system extending onto caudal fin; high arching back; subterminal mouth; conjoined spinous and soft dorsal fins, and ability to make loud booming sounds by contracting muscles along the walls of the gas bladder. Caudal fin triangular.
**Habitat** Deep pools of medium to large rivers and large impoundments.
**Range** Entire Mississippi River system, north to Hudson Bay drainage in Manitoba and southwestern Saskatchewan.

# Cichlids – Cichlidae

This large family is native to Africa, Central and South America. One species, the Rio Grande perch, ranges northward into Texas. Family characters include an interrupted lateral line and one aperature for each nostril.

## Rio Grande cichlid
*Cichlasoma cyanoguttatum*                    12in (30cm)

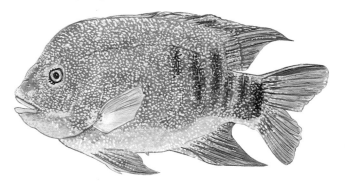

**Identification** A deep-bodied, compressed, brownish fish with a curved dorsal profile, single nostril on each side of snout, dorsal fins joint. Sides with bluish to whitish spots and four to six bars. Dorsal and anal fins pointed posteriorly. Anal fin with five to six spines. Lateral line interrupted with 27–30 scales in lateral series.
**Habitat** Backwater vegetated areas of warm streams.
**Range** Rio Grande, Texas to New Mexico in Gulf of Mexico drainage.

# Mullets – Mugilidae

Mullets are primarily marine fishes found worldwide, although several species, such as the striped mullet, enter fresh water. Mullets are characterized by high pectoral fins, adipose eyelids, spinous dorsal fin with four spines placed well forward of the soft dorsal and small, weak mouth.

## Striped mullet
*Mugil cephalus*                                    36in (91cm)

**Identification** Blunt snout; flat head; two well-separated dorsal fins, highly placed pectoral fins; adipose eyelids. Sides with six to seven dark horizontal stripes.
**Habitat** Generally coastal and estuarine areas; but enters fresh water.
**Range** Atlantic Ocean from Cape Cod to South America including Gulf of Mexico; Pacific Ocean from San Francisco Bay to South America.

# Sculpins – Cottidae

Primarily a marine family, many species of this family are restricted to fresh water. Members of this group are characterized by large flattened heads, expanded pectoral fins, naked bodies, eyes dorsal in position on sides of head, and tapering posterior portion of the body.

## Sharpnose sculpin
*Clinocottus acuticeps*                                     2in (5cm)

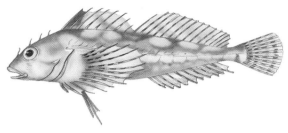

**Identification** Distinctive, flattened tripartite anal papilla; cirri on the eyeballs, head, lateral line and at tip of each dorsal spine. Three dark lines radiating from the eye.
**Habitat** Marine; occasionally enters fresh water.
**Range** Pacific Coast, from Big Sur River, California north along the coast of Alaska.

# Coastrange sculpin
*Cottus aleuticus*                                    3in (7.6cm)

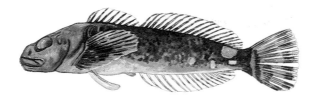

**Identification**  Single pore on tip of chin, no palatine teeth, and no
pronounced gap between first and second dorsal fins. Two to three
dark saddle-like blotches below soft dorsal fin. Dark bars on fins.
Lateral line pores 34–44.
**Habitat**  Coastal streams in swift riffles.
**Range**  Pacific Coast from California north to Aleutian Islands.

# Prickly sculpin
*Cottus asper*                                        3½in (9cm)

**Identification**  Single pore at tip of chin; 15–19 anal fin rays, palatine
teeth, lateral line pores, 32–43. Three bars or blotches below soft
dorsal. Fins with dark bars. First dorsal with dark spot toward rear.
**Habitat**  Coastal streams.
**Range**  Pacific Coast from Ventura River, California, northward to
Seward, Alaska.

# Mottled sculpin
*Cottus bairdi*

4in (10cm)

**Identification** Caudal peduncle deep and naked body. Body with dark mottling; dark saddles below dorsal fin. First dorsal fin in males black, tipped with orange. Lateral line incomplete, with 18–25 pores.
**Habitat** Moderate-sized, clear, cold streams, rivers and lakes over rock and gravel bottoms.
**Range** Extending from Quebec to Ontario and Manitoba south to Georgia, west to Missouri; Alberta and British Columbia west to Oregon, Utah, Colorado and south to New Mexico.

# Banded sculpin
*Cottus carolinae*

8in (20cm)

**Identification** Large eyes and mouth. Naked body. Three black dorsal saddles extending down sides. Preopercle with sharp spine. Chin mottled. Lateral line complete, 30 or more pores.
**Habitat** Riffles of clear, gravel-bottomed streams and rivers in swift current.
**Range** Southeastern USA from West Virginia and Georgia to Kansas and Oklahoma.

# Slimy sculpin
*Cottus cognatus*                                          4in (10cm)

**Identification** Caudal peduncle slender. Chin lightly pigmented.
Base of first dorsal fin dark with a clear edge. Anal rays usually 11–12.
Three preopercular spines. Lateral line incomplete, ends at middle of
second dorsal fin.
**Habitat** Springs, clear, cold, high gradient gravel and rock-bottomed
streams; also in rocky shoal areas of lakes.
**Range** Alaska and Canada, Great Lakes south to Virginia, Maine to
Oregon.

# Ozark sculpin
*Cottus hypselurus*                                      4½in (11cm)

**Identification** Wedge-shaped, naked body. Three dark saddles cross
dorsum. Median fins mottled. Basicaudal bar generally with a straight
posterior edge. Chin uniformly pigmented. Lateral line incomplete,
19–26 pores. Dorsal fins broadly joined.
**Habitat** Cool, clear, swift streams and riffles of rivers over gravel
substrates.
**Range** Northern Arkansas and southern Missouri.

# Torrent sculpin
*Cottus rhothecus*

3in (7.6cm)

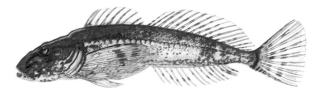

**Identification** Two pores on tip of chin; prickles on sides and back. Two dark saddles beneath second dorsal fin extending forward. Palatine teeth present. Lateral line with more than 30 pores, reaching past last ray of second dorsal fin.
**Habitat** Swift riffles of large streams and rivers.
**Range** Lower Columbia River and Puget Sound drainage.

# Deepwater sculpin
*Myoxocephalus thompsoni*

8in (20cm)

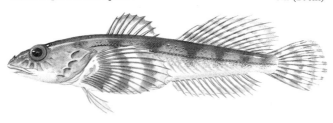

**Identification** Head distinctly flattened dorsoventrally; slender caudal peduncle. Gill membranes meet at an acute angle. Dorsal fins not joined, separated. Four preopercular spines (upper two appearing as one large bifurate spine).
**Habitat** Deep, cold, inland lakes.
**Range** Circumpolar in distribution; Canada south to Great Lakes.

# Index